TRUE DECEIT FALSE LOVE

Simple Explanations for Complex Terms on Domestic Violence, Narcissistic Abuse, Parental Alienation & Intergenerational Family Trauma

Dr. Marni Hill Foderaro

BALBOA.PRESS
A DIVISION OF HAY HOUSE

Balboa Press books may be ordered through booksellers or by contacting:

Balboa Press
A Division of Hay House
1663 Liberty Drive
Bloomington, IN 47403
www.balboapress.com
844-682-1282

ISBN: 979-8-7652-4744-0 (sc)
ISBN: 979-8-7652-4743-3 (e)

Library of Congress Control Number: 2023922066

Print information available on the last page.

Balboa Press rev. date: 02/05/2024

CONTENTS

Dedication vii
Author Biography.. viii
Preface xiii
Disclaimer... xxv
Introduction... xxxi
Terms xxxv

A... 1
B... 11
C... 17
D... 29
E.. 39
F.. 47
G...55
H... 59
I...65
J.. 71
K.. 75
L... 77
M... 83
N...91
O... 97
P..101
Q..113
R..115
S..123
T..137
U..143
V..147
W...151
X..155
Y..157
Z..159

"Whatever words we utter should be chosen with care, for people will hear them and be influenced by them for good or ill."
~ Buddha

This 7th volume in my prominently endorsed, multi-book series
TRUE DECEIT FALSE LOVE
Simple Explanations for Complex Terms
is dedicated to the Victims and Survivors of Domestic Violence, Narcissistic Abuse, Parental Alienation and Intergenerational Family Trauma. Bringing awareness is especially needed for the young and adult, innocent, Alienated Children who are strategically used as destructive weapons to unjustly reject, fear, blame, disparage and cut off their Targeted, normal-range Loving Parent and their entire side of that family. These Abused Children are unknowingly aligned with, brainwashed, dependent on and Trauma-Bonded with the calculating, malevolent, mentally unstable manipulator, the other Alienating Parent, and his/her regime. The damage caused to all Victims by the Abusing Alienators has devastating and negative life-long consequences. My heart goes out to all of the men, women, children and extended family members who have experienced this extreme form of Intimate Partner Violence and Family Terrorism. I sincerely believe in my heart that even though justice does not always triumph over evil and wrongdoing, that truth, love, compassion and goodness will and does eventually prevail. Evil darkness will not outshine love and light.

AUTHOR

BIOGRAPHY

www.GodCameToMyGarageSale.com

Dr. Marni Hill Foderaro is a multi-award-winning and celebrated author, speaker and educator. She earned her doctorate in education from Northern Illinois University and completed postdoctoral studies at Harvard during a very successful and rewarding 35-year career as a high school special education teacher, with 12 years as a university graduate school adjunct professor. Marni's life was forever changed after experiencing numerous trauma-induced STEs-Spiritually Transformative Encounters. Marni's 2022 Hollywood Book Fest runner-up, 2020 Best Books finalist Award Winning and 5-Star Reader's Favorite Spiritual fiction, inspired by true events, *"GOD CAME TO MY GARAGE SALE"* is prominently endorsed by James Redfield, best selling author of *"The Celestine Prophecy"* series of books, and other notables in the Spiritual community, including founding directors of IANDS (International Association for Near Death Studies). Marni's latest prominently endorsed multi-book series entitled: *"TRUE DECEIT FALSE LOVE"* creatively addresses and provides tools and resources for understanding and healing from Domestic Violence, Narcissistic Abuse, Parental Alienation and Intergenerational Family Trauma. Marni is a lover of animals, nature, music and world travel who handles life's challenges with love and compassion. She values honesty, integrity, equality and goodness and prays for peace on earth. Marni was born in the South, raised her children in the Midwest and lives in the Caribbean. In addition to her TV/podcast interviews, speaking engagements and various writing endeavors on embracing Spirituality after surviving Domestic Violence, Narcissistic Abuse, Parental Alienation and Intergenerational Family Trauma, Marni is a contributing author to numerous anthology books, including: *"The Last Breath," "The Evolution of Echo," "We're All In This Together: Embrace One Another," "Passing The Pearls," "Write & Publish Your Book," "The Ulti-MUTT Book for Dog Lovers"* and *"bLU Talks Presents"* (*Business, Life and the Universe.*) In 2022 Dr. Marni Hill Foderaro was inducted into the Bestselling Authors International (BAI) Organization.

"Sticks and stones may break our bones,
but words will break our hearts."
~ Robert Fulghum

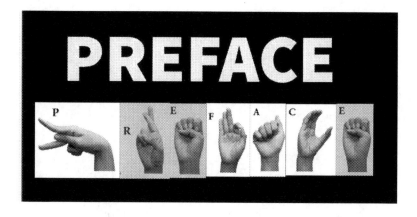

A Heartfelt Note From The Author

When you eventually realize that you have been the Target of Domestic Violence, Narcissistic Abuse, Parental Alienation and/or Intergenerational Family Trauma at the hands of someone you cared for and trusted with unconditional love, in some cases unknowingly enduring this Intimate Partner Terrorism for decades, your entire world is turned upside down.

After the initial shock of realizing that you ignored years of glaring Red Flags as you were significantly betrayed and deceitfully manipulated, you muster up the courage to escape in the hopes that you can reclaim your life before it's too late. You acknowledge that there are huge repercussions to leaving your Abuser. Life as you knew it will never be the same. Your mind races as you now have to consider your basic safety and survival needs of food, shelter, money, transportation and employment. There are family ties for most, and we must contemplate the consequences and impact of our choices on others, especially our immediate family and children.

Some of us are forced to stay because we lack the inner strength or resources to escape, are afraid of or don't think we are capable of making such a drastic change or we have young children with our Abuser and instinctively must look out for our children's safety and wellbeing. Other Victims take time to carefully get their situations and assets in order so that they have a better chance at a more comfortable exit. Many of us just follow our gut instincts and knee-jerk reactions, using our best judgment and remove ourselves from the toxic situation and separate ourselves from the Abusive person and environment at our earliest chance, leaving without a well-thought-out plan.

Abusers and Alienators are Predators and they don't usually let their Targeted Prey or Victims go easily or without a fight. The Abuser's need to keep up their False Public Persona by Smearing and Abusing their Victim can go on for years and even decades. Their malevolence is actually entertainment for them as they enjoy the power, control, chaos and confrontations. Most of these destructive individuals have traits of Mental Illness and if they would ever seek professional help or diagnosis for their condition, a medical, psychological or psychiatric practitioner might label them as a Cluster B Personality Disordered Covert Malignant Narcissist, Psychopath and/or Sociopath. No two Abusers are alike as each person's behavior and personality falls on a spectrum of severity.

Most of these Abusers want to punish, discredit and destroy their Targets, especially when the truth of the Abuser's behaviors, deceit and lack of integrity may be exposed. However, they all seem to feel that they are above the law and that society's rules don't apply to them; that's why they are so immoral, cutthroat and dishonest. They believe in their false perceived power of superiority. Somehow they all follow the same general playbook, so their extremely vindictive behaviors are often textbook predictable.

Significant harm is caused to innocent Victims as these scheming Abusers are known to methodically Gaslight their Targets for years. These Abusers mirror your positive traits and values because they are like empty vessels who lack empathy and morals, yet strive to fit into the mainstream to carry out their dirty and devious deeds. In the beginning of the relationship they state that they value and care about all of the same things that you do. You are put on a pedestal as the Love Bombing and Future Faking sucks you into the illusion that you have finally met your soulmate. You pinch yourself because the relationship seems too good to be true. You don't see the Bait-and-Hook strategy. You may believe that you are living in a fairytale, and you eventually and comfortably settle into living the coveted "American Dream."

Over time, however, you begin to feel confused and experience bouts of Cognitive Dissonance as the Abuser acts one way around others, flaunting their created Public Persona to maintain their False Image, and another way with you behind closed doors. You may begin to doubt yourself, your discernment or your abilities. Your physical health suffers and you may develop autoimmune diseases because slowly, without you knowing it, your body and mind have been in "fight or flight" survival mode. Eventually your identity and perspectives are so fundamentally distorted due to the inflicted Trauma that you lose your previously solid confidence and find yourself dependent on your Abuser as he/she now has the authority over the purse strings and everything in your environment, including who you can see, what you can do and where and when you can go. Your Abuser's controlling actions do not match his/her words. You are trapped and stifled with little or no freedom, but you accept your circumstances because these constraints are presented under the cloak of care and concern for your wellbeing. You believe them when they tell you that they care about you and are always looking out for your best interest. Besides, you are busy focusing on your job, home and family and have invested so much time and commitment to this relationship that you plug along thinking and trusting that things will get better as you hope for the best while you continue to honor the vows you made under God.

These calculating Perpetrators begin to accuse you and others of their own wrongdoings and unethical or illegal activities. Behind your back, they Smear your name to everyone and anyone in your circle with outlandish lies and believable half-truths. They gain support and sympathy by playing the Victim to people who end up being Flying Monkeys, doing the bidding and spying for the Abuser. These Abusers are Alienators who Brainwash your children, family, friends, neighbors, coworkers and countless others in cult-like fashion to believe that you are a bad or sick person who should be avoided and feared. They accuse their Targets of cheating, stealing and lying, when the reality is that they are the ones cheating, stealing and lying. These ruthless bullies lack empathy and engage in Projection which is done with such careful planning and malevolent intent, setting the stage for when the relationship will eventually dissolve, either through a planned or unexpected Discard or your untimely death. In addition to their numerous extramarital escapades, these Secret Agents keep in contact with old flames and are always on the prowl to line up replacement relationships in their Harem Closet in the event that they choose to Discard you as their main source of supply, or worse yet for the Abuser, you become wise to their games, choose to leave them to cautiously carry out your escape.

It's usually not until after you separate from the Abuser that you realize you are left with no support system or money; your lifelong friends and long-term neighbors become Flying Monkeys for the Abuser and give you the cold shoulder, wanting nothing to do with you anymore. It's shocking because you thought that these close relationships were strong and you took for granted that they would always be there for you. In stealth fashion, the Abusers utilize the Divide and Conquer method and focus their Campaign of Denigration on those closest to us, so even your relationships with your family members and best friends surprisingly change as well. These revengeful and vindictive Perpetrators fear being exposed and their False Public Persona and malevolent intentions and actions revealed to the masses who they've fooled for years. Justice does not usually seem to prevail for the Targeted Victims as the family court system is often part of the problem, but if you escape and do the research, inner reflection and Shadow Work, you have a great chance of moving forward, starting over with rebuilding your life and eventually finding peace, harmony and true love.

Abusers are also obsessed with stealing and manipulating money and are often fiscally irresponsible as they create extensive debt and chaotic financial calculations on their professional-looking spreadsheets. For Discovery, they lie on their reporting of monies due and assets owned so that the "ratio", which is then used throughout the entire divorce/ judgment process, is inaccurate and misleading, ensuring that they come out financially way ahead of the Targeted, soon-to-be ex spouse. Years later the Targets realize that they have been financially abused all along. Most Victims find that their cash and assets have been suddenly depleted and their house goes into foreclosure even when for years they were told and believed that the family home was paid off. The Victim learns that all of the joint charge cards are maxed out and new credit cards were fraudulently opened up with their forged name and social security number. These Abusers illegally engage in Identity Theft and even steal their own kids' money from their bank accounts, empty their college funds, cash in their savings bonds and take out credit cards in their children's names without them ever knowing. It's not until years later that you may find out that the Abusers's urgent need for large sums of cash is to fund their dubious double or triple life of pornography, gambling and/or substance abuse addictions, private investments, hidden assets or even to support another family or love-children they never disclosed to you; many Adult Children are shocked to later find out that they have half-siblings that were secretly kept from them. Most of these Adult Children never find out the truth because they are Trauma Bonded and out of fear and obligation, stay aligned with their lying, Abusing, Alienating Parent their entire life.

A very common coping mechanism for the Victims who are courageous enough to escape the Abusive Relationship is to try to make sense of how and why such bad things can happen to such good people. You, as the honest Empath who was betrayed, are compelled to play the role of detective as you begin to seek information and confirmation though your own investigations using computer searches, literature research, books, blogs, YouTube videos, podcasts and therapeutic counseling. You try to get answers to your many questions in an attempt to put a name to your feelings and experiences. You quickly find that you are not alone and that there is a huge support network out there of professionals and everyday people who have experienced Domestic Violence, Narcissistic Abuse, Parental Alienation and Intergenerational Family Trauma, and often, as part of their own healing process, are driven to provide awareness, resources and support to others.

Recovering from the extreme Complex Trauma and stress of this type of Abuse is a process and takes a great deal of time. Victims are forced to navigate through significant shock and loss as they experience each of the stages of grief: shock/denial, pain/guilt, anger/bargaining, sadness, regaining hope, acceptance and growth. You may have been able to move on or move far away to reclaim your life and start over, but you continue to be haunted by your experiences and dashed hopes for your future. Most of us have to deal with breaking Trauma Bonds and our Abuser's continued emotional, physical or legal stalking and harassment for years, in extreme cases, even decades. Abusers enjoy taking you back to court and forcing you to engage in "law-fare." Making sure that you must spend thousands of dollars to engage in defending yourself with their bad faith petitions is often the only way that your Abusive Ex-Spouse can stay connected to you. They become obsessed with you and your demise, just like their other addictions. They are the ones left with a great deal of money to misuse the justice system in frivolous lawsuits against you. They love the feeling of being dominant over their Victim as they deplete your time, energy, money and resources. You may feel alone and lonely as your support system has vanished, although in time, this period of Isolation can prove to be helpful as you quietly regain your independence and inner strength.

During your recovery efforts of self-healing and self-love and to understand your role in this unfortunate situation, it is helpful to reflect on and examine your family of origin dynamics and acknowledge your own childhood Traumas, Abandonment issues, Core Wounds and probable Intergenerational Abuse that most likely contributed to your naivety and unmet emotional needs which eventually lead you to choosing toxic, controlling and Abusive partnerships and friendships. This history may have also contributed to you trusting too much too soon, being an over-giver, peoplepleaser or having weak boundaries, making you the perfect Target for your Abuser.

You probably came across this book as a result of your quest for knowledge on this topic. Well, I'm glad you did and hopefully the timing was synchronistic with where you are at in your terminology inquiry and healing journey. This resource of over 1,000 terms with easy-to-understand definitions, *TRUE DECEIT FALSE LOVE Simple Explanations for Complex Terms on Domestic Violence, Narcissistic Abuse, Parental Alienation & Intergenerational Family Trauma,* will hopefully provide you with much needed information and validation. Just reading through the very short and to-the-point definitions in this book will give you the awareness to the plethora of words and simple explanations associated with much of what you may have experienced. This list is by no means complete and new verbiage is being created daily. I take absolutely no credit in the development of any of these commonly-used terms as they have been coined by countless others and are regularly circulated amongst the Abuse Recovery Community. This is not a detailed, traditional glossary or dictionary either. There are numerous and varied meanings and definitions for each word; to include them all in this volume would be too overwhelming and frankly, at the same time, too limiting. I just used my years of personal experience and research to come up with my own basic explanations, as if I was trying to define this community's vernacular to a friend or fellow Victim/Survivor. Also, doing your own research of looking up other meanings to these words while you are simultaneously connecting the dots to your own experiences can be very therapeutic and an integral part of the healing process and your personal growth.

In closing, I would like to offer hope and encouragement to all of the men, women, children and families who find themselves navigating Domestic Violence, Narcissistic Abuse, Parental Alienation and/or Intergenerational Family Trauma. Know that you are a beautiful, loving soul who should be treated with kindness and respect. You are not crazy. You didn't do anything to deserve the malicious treatment you previously received or are currently receiving at the hands of your Abusing spouse, friend, acquaintance, neighbor, colleague, boss, coach, therapist, parent, adult child and/or extended family member and their aligned cohorts. Don't be hard on yourself that it took you so long to finally see things for what they really are; Abusers are very calculating and skilled Master Manipulators who put great efforts into hiding their covert venomous, vindictive and vile deceit behind their Fraudulent Mask. Remember, nobody is perfect and we are all here to grow as individuals as we learn life's lessons. You know the truth and the facts of what you've been through.

Try to look objectively at what has happened to you so you can unlearn negative patterns and steer away from unhealthy tendencies as you become more vigilant in recognizing Abusive people and situations, while understanding yourself more. The family, friends, neighbors, coworkers and acquaintances that you lose because you no longer resonate with them, their behavior or values, make room for new relationships with like-minded people of integrity. Watch out for the Hoovers, as Abusers often return to re-engage with their original Supply. Be willing to change and get out of your comfort zone.

Reflect on the values that are meaningful to you and stay true to them. Honor who you are. Acknowledge your feelings. Manage the Triggers, as there will be many things and situations that will keep you stuck and traumatized. Choose to respond, not react, to life's challenges. Embrace your authenticity as you gather up your strength to strive for independence and personal growth while you get back on your feet. You have what it takes to get through this. Knowledge is power.

Understanding yourself, as well as learning the dynamics and related terms to describe your experiences with toxic individuals who engage in Domestic Violence, Narcissistic Abuse, Parental Alienation and/or Intergenerational Family Trauma can be very enlightening and help empower you to move towards peace and Self-Actualization. You need to take responsibility for your role, foundational patterns and Trauma Bonds which made you a perfect Target for Abuse. You must change, as you cannot and should not ever go back to how things were. You are stronger than you know. Your Survivor Voice matters. Turn your negative experiences into positive opportunities to evolve into the genuine person that you were meant to be. Don't be surprised if you experience some type of Spiritual Awakening and are now more in tune with the universe's signs and synchronicities. Have faith. This may be a good time to reconnect with, embrace and trust in a Higher Source.

You never know, God could even come to your garage sale!

My sincere hope is that the simple explanations for complex terms in this 7th volume of my prominently endorsed, multi-book series *"TRUE DECEIT FALSE LOVE"* will provide you with much needed information and validation. Stay strong as you take back your power to live a beautiful and fulfilling life. You deserve more and the best is yet to come. Truth eventually prevails.

I wish you compassion, goodness and peace on your Healing Journey. Much love and light to you.

Many Blessings Always,
Marni

TRUE DECEIT FALSE LOVE

Simple Explanations for Complex Terms
on Domestic Violence, Narcissistic Abuse, Parental Alienation
& Intergenerational Family Trauma

Realizing that you have endured Domestic Violence, Narcissistic Abuse, Parental Alienation and/or Intergenerational Family Trauma, and finding the words to help you understand and articulate what you've been through can be exceptionally challenging.

Language has the power to hurt,
but language also has the power to heal.

This unique and ingenious reference book,
TRUE DECEIT FALSE LOVE
Simple Explanations for Complex Terms
is a must-have resource. Learning the vocabulary helps you connect-the dots to your own experiences and can be extremely therapeutic on your Healing Journey. In time, the Abuser's Mask Slips and with your own research and reflection, you will come to understand the truth, find your Survivor's Voice and reclaim your life.

"You never know when a moment and a few sincere words can have an impact on a life."
~ Zig Ziglar

The simple explanations for the complex terms provided in this book are on an "as is" basis and intended for informational, educational and entertainment purposes only, and should not be understood to constitute a medical, psychological or psychiatric diagnosis, healthcare recommendation or legal advice. The author's intent is to build awareness and provide linguistic examples to understand and heal from the trauma of experiencing Domestic Violence, Narcissistic Abuse, Parental Alienation and Intergenerational Family Trauma. The author and publisher make no representations or warranties of any kind with respect to the contents in this book and assume no responsibility for errors, inaccuracies, omissions or any other inconsistencies herein. Reading these terms and phrases are at your own risk and you agree to take full responsibility for any resulting consequences. The information in this book is not a substitution for direct expert assistance and may be triggering. Please seek legal advice or professional help from a medical, psychological, psychiatric or healthcare specialist if necessary. The author did not develop any these terms and explanations, as they were coined by countless others, and is not an expert or licensed provider on Domestic Violence, Narcissistic Abuse, Parental Alienation or Intergenerational Family Trauma, is not responsible for any resulting consequences, and the use of this book implies your acceptance of this disclaimer.

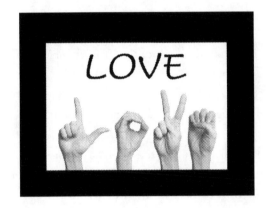

"False words are not only evil in themselves,
but they infect the soul with evil."
~ Socrates

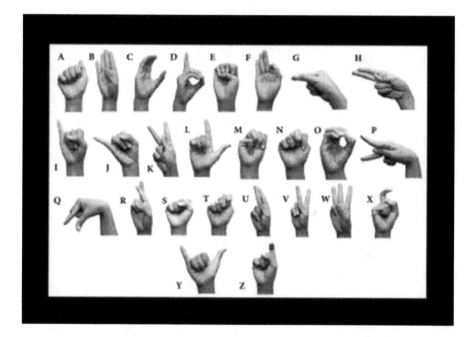

"Words - so innocent and powerless as they are, as standing in a dictionary, how potent for good and evil they become in the hands of one who knows how to combine them."
~ Nathaniel Hawthorne

INTRODUCTION

By Anoushka Marcin

Understanding the terminology used by the narcissistic abuse community is crucial for several reasons. Primarily, it empowers survivors of narcissistic abuse to articulate their experiences and feelings accurately. This language provides them with the tools to validate their own struggles and connect with others who have faced similar challenges, reducing feelings of isolation and self-doubt. Next, knowledge of this terminology aids mental health professionals in recognising and addressing narcissistic abuse. This can lead to more effective therapy and support for survivors, helping them on their path to recovery. Further, awareness of the narcissistic abuse lexicon can contribute to broader societal understanding of this pervasive issue. The more people are educated about the dynamics and tactics employed by narcissists, the better equipped they are to identify abusive behaviour in their own lives, potentially preventing further harm. In essence, the knowledge of terminology within the narcissistic abuse community serves as a valuable tool for survivors, therapists, and society as a whole. It fosters empathy, support, and a collective effort to combat narcissistic abuse, ultimately promoting healing, resilience, and healthier relationships.

I am a motivational speaker and online presence talking about narcissism and emotional trauma. I am a trainee psychologist and my work is about enabling the survivor to realise that recovery is possible by reconnecting back to themselves and starting to build a strong alliance with their core spirit. This is a very important and necessary part of the process of healing. My work has reached audiences of millions around the globe through my thought provoking and enlightening videos, wellbeing blogs and social media posts.

I met Marni a few years ago when she began writing her prominently endorsed and very well received **_TRUE DECEIT FALSE LOVE_** book series which provides terminology, tools and a creative approach to understanding and healing from Domestic Violence, Narcissistic Abuse, Parental Alienation and Intergenerational Family Trauma. We clicked the moment we met; you see, Marni values honesty and has a warm, compassionate and authentic disposition, which I would say is not typical nowadays. Some people are like a rare diamond and when you meet them, you want to keep connected to their kindness. Marni is a rare diamond and I feel blessed that our paths crossed. Through this dark subject that we both are well versed in, I hope that our friendship, along with our respective outreach efforts, can provide inspiration to others so they will know that there are genuine, empathetic and authentic people in the world. You just need to set and enforce healthy boundaries in relationships when your gut intuition tells you to pay attention to red flags, while you educate yourself, learn the many "simple explanations for complex terms," acknowledge and take ownership of your foundational patterns, prioritize your wellbeing and make true connections with people of integrity.

I cannot praise Marni enough for her writing and what she brings to survivors to be able to put to words their experiences. These covert and dark experiences are intentionally kept in the shadows by the malevolent perpetrators and their accomplices. Many survivors do not have the linguistic vocabulary to describe what has happened to them. Through Marni's work, she sheds light onto such a hidden and emotive subject, enabling survivors to be able to articulate what they've been through, which allows empowerment out of victimhood. There is no-one else like Marni who, with her work and collections, has provided such unique, supportive and compassionate tools to help the reader understand Domestic Violence, Narcissistic Abuse, Parental Alienation, Intergenerational Family Trauma and Best Friend Betrayal and empower them with the vernacular to move forward in renewed hope. And hope is what every survivor needs to be able to step into a new chapter of their lives.

I give my highest praise to Dr. Marni Hill Foderaro for bringing such impactful resources to a much needed topic with her book series, **_TRUE DECEIT FALSE LOVE_**

~Anoushka Marcin
Motivational Speaker, Trainee Psychologist, well-being Coach, self-development Workshop Facilitator, YouTube/livestream vlogger, writer of SELF GENERATION: The Restoration of You, featured inspirational interview @ BBC, Owner of @balance.psychologies

Website: askanoushka.co.uk
Mentorship: patron.com/askanoushka
YouTube: youtube.com/@anoushkamarcin
Social Media Links: instagram.com/anoushkamarcin tiktok.com/@askanoushka facebook.com/askanoushka twitter.com/AnoushkaMarcin

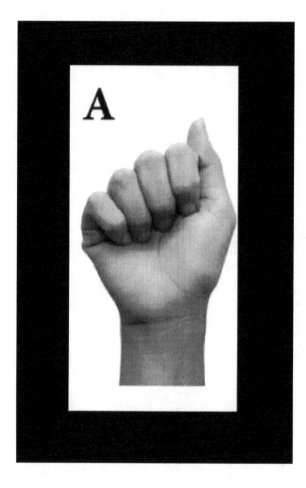

ACE-Adverse Childhood Experiences-

Experiencing traumatic events of Abuse, neglect and early dysfunction that impact someone as an adult

ACoN-Adult Children of Narcissists-

If you grew up with a Narcissistic Parent

Abandonment-

When you feel undesired, ignored, left behind or Discarded

Abandonment Wounds-

Feelings of loss when your Abuser Discards, Devalues or Dismisses you

Abduction-

When an Alienating Parent kidnaps the child(ren)

Above the Law-

Narcissists believe that they can get away with illegal activities and wrongdoing because they think they are special and societal rules don't apply to them

Absent Parent-

A parent who is not around to raise the child(ren)

Abuse-

When someone hurts, insults, injures or sexually molests another. Abuse can be physical, emotional, verbal, financial, sexual or spiritual

Abuse Amnesia-

Target's lack of memory and/or denial that they have been treated poorly from the Abuser

Abuse By Proxy-

When the Abuser uses another person to Abuse the Victim/Target on their behalf

Abuse Community-
Group of advocates, influencers, researchers, coaches, therapists and Survivors who provide support to Victims of Domestic Violence, Narcissistic Abuse, Parental Alienation and/or Intergenerational Family Trauma

Abuse Cycle-
The persistence and cyclical pattern of physically and/or emotionally battering another. Phases of the Abuse Cycle can be described as Honeymoon, Tension Build Up and Violence or Idealization, Devaluing and/or Discard

Abuse Excuse-
When an Abuser blames his/her prior Trauma for his/her current violent acts against others

Abuse Tactic-
Strategy used by a malevolent person wanting to cause harm to a Target

Abuser-
Person who is committing the harmful acts to another

Abusive Punishment-
The use of excessive physical force to discipline a child(ren) or other Targeted person that results in bodily injury

Access Blocking-
When an Alienating Parent refuses visitation or communication between the child(ren) and the Targeted Parent

Accusations-
Statements made to place blame on another. Narcissists and Alienators often use Projection to make False Accusations against the Victim or Target to discredit them

Acrimonious Divorce-
A legal separation characterized by bitterness, where one spouse has treated the other so badly that any type of reconciliation is impossible

Acting Out-
Behavioral expression of emotions to relieve tension, including arguing, threatening, fighting and/or being aggressive

Actor-
The false role the Narcissist, Abuser or Alienator plays to create an illusion, pretending to be someone that they are not

Acute Stress/Anxiety-
Sudden feeling of dread and apprehension after experiencing a Traumatic situation

Acute Trauma-
A one-time event of Abuse

Adapted Child-
When a child, in response to Abuse or Alienation, is compliant and orderly, yet manipulative

Addict-
A person who has developed a compulsion or dependence on drugs, substances or activities

Addicted-
A person who has an unhealthy reliance on substances, behaviors, pornography, sex and/or gambling

Addiction-
The state of psychological and/or physical dependence on alcohol, drugs, behaviors, pornography, sex, food and/or gambling

Adjustment Disorder-
Stress, feelings of sadness or hopelessness and even physical symptoms that happen after experiencing stress or Abuse

Adult Narcissistic Children-
When your offspring develop entitled, self-centered and/or Abusive traits of Narcissism, much like their Alienating Parent

Adultery-
When your spouse or partner cheats and has an emotional or physical affair with another person

Adultify-
The inappropriate and harmful treatment of a child as if they were an adult

Advocate-
A trained professional or volunteer that helps Targeted Victims

Affairs-
Cheating and emotional/physical infidelity while one is married or in a partnership

Aftermath-
The inevitable fallout consequences resulting from divorce or separation, often instigated by the Abuser or Alienator

Aggressive Parenting-
When a parent uses physical or emotional threats or punishment to control or pressure their child(ren) to obey their rules or orders

Aggressive-Rejected Child-
A child who is prone to hostile, reactive and antagonistic behavior toward others

Aggressor-
The person who attacks another first

Aging Narcissist-
A person who becomes more and more Narcissistic as they get older

Aliases-
The many fake names or personas that Abusers use to hide their true identity

Alienated-
The emotional, physical and unjustified cut-off of someone by the influence of another

Alienated Parent-
The Loving Parent whose relationship with their child(ren) has been interfered with, undermined, damaged and/or disrupted without a valid reason or justification, usually as punishment of the Targeted Victim for leaving the Abusing Spouse or Partner

Alienating Parent-
The Abusing Parent who causes a child to unjustifiably fear, reject, badmouth and/or sever ties with their other loving, Normal-Range Parent

Alienation-
When the Abusing Parent influences the child(ren) to reject, denigrate, fear and/or sever ties with the other Loving Parent, when there has been no Abuse or neglect that would warrant this

Alienator-
The Abusing Person who gets the child(ren) to align with them and hate, fear or cut off their Loving Parent based on a False Narrative of lies and believable Half-Truths

Alienator's Recruits-
The people, often called Flying Monkeys, who the Abusing Alienator gets to align with and act on their distorted narrative

Aligned Child-
The Abused Child(ren) who are loyal to the Alienating, Narcissistic Parent out of fear of abandonment or being coerced or bought off

Alimony-
The financial court-ordered support given to a spouse by the other spouse following a divorce

All-Bad Parent-
The Loving, Normal-Range, Targeted Parent who is perceived by the child(ren) to be 100% negative

All-Good Parent-
The Abusive, Manipulative, Alienating Parent who is perceived by the child(ren) to be 100% positive

Allegations-
A statement declaring someone has done something wrong, harmful and/or illegal

Allegiance-
When someone is aligned with and is in full support of another

Alligator Tears-
Fake crying to elicit sympathy from others

Allostatic Load-
Cumulative wear-and-tear resulting from repeated efforts to understand your Abuse and your trying to adapt to the stress and/or adversity over time

Ally-
Person who supports another

Altruism-
Unselfish behavior that benefits others without egoistic motivation

Altruistic Narcissist-
A Narcissist who comes across as unselfish and caring of others, when they are not

Ambient Abuse-
When you are constantly exposed to an exploitative Abuser who belittles, Gaslights, controls, manipulates and is hostile and emotionally oppressive causing the Target to lose confidence and independence

Ambiguous Loss-
Loss that occurs without closure or understanding, leaving the Victim searching for answers and struggling with acceptance or unresolved grief. This happens after a Narcissistic Discard or experiencing Parental Alienation

Amends Letter-
An apology letter that a Targeted Parent writes to their Alienated Child to acknowledge their behavior in the hopes of reconnecting or reunifying

Ammunition-
Information and tactics used by the Abuser to cause harm to their Targeted Victim

Amputated Parent-
A parent who has been Erased, cut-off or removed from a child's life by an Alienating Parent

Anchoring Effects/Errors-
When thoughts about people or situations are influenced by your first impressions

Anger-
Emotion when you are upset and vehemently opposed to someone's words and/or actions

Annulment-
Court ruling that a marriage was never valid, resulting from fraud or misrepresentation

Antagonistic Narcissist-
A very Manipulative and Aggressive Narcissist who is very competitive and starts conflicts and/or fights

Antisocial-
Person who disregards social norms or laws

Antisocial Personality Disorder-ASPD-
Presence of a chronic and pervasive disregard to violate other's rights, including breaking the law, exploitation, deceitfulness, impulsivity, aggression and/or irresponsibility with a lack of guilt, remorse or empathy

Anxiety-
When you feel uneasy due to fear, stress and/or Abuse

Anxiety Disorder-
Any group of disorders related to the emotional states of fear, worry, stress or excessive apprehension

Apathy-
Also called Lack of Empathy and is the inability to consider the emotional state of others. Classic characteristic of Narcissists

Appeasing-
To pacify or placate someone or something by giving into their demands

Armchair Psychologist-
Psychological inquiry based on introspection and rational thought without empirical case study

Assault and Battery-
The wrong and threatening act of causing emotional fear and physical harm to another

Attachment Disorder-
Disruption in the developmental patterns related to social interactions due to Abuse and/or neglect from a caregiver

Attachment System-
The psychological theory related to connections between a parent/caregiver and the child(ren)

Atychiphobia-
Fear of making mistakes

Authentic Self-
Being genuine and free to be yourself and follow your own interests and values

Authorities-
Legal or high-ranking people and/or experts who make or enforce standards or laws

Avoidance-
The action of not doing something or staying away from a person or situation

Avoidant Personality Disorder-
Hypersensitivity to rejection and criticism, withdrawing due to low self-esteem and stress

Awakened-
Aware, no longer ignoring or not acknowledging reality

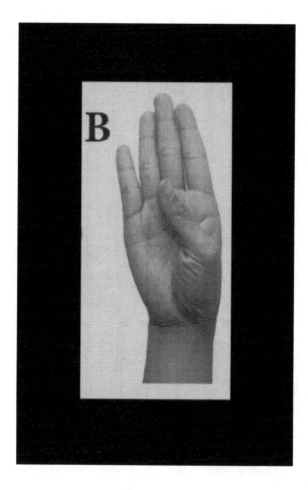

BITE Model-
Controls used by Alienators and Cult Leaders to Gaslight their Targets, which include: **B**ehavior, **I**nformation, **T**houghts and **E**motions

Back Up Supply-
The Abuser's next-in-line relationship, when and if there are problems with his/her current "A" relationship or Primary Supply

Backhanded Compliment-
Kind and complimentary comments given to another that are really not sincere, and could be said to elicit reciprocal compliments

Backstabber-
A person who betrays the trust of another, by making negative comments or claims without the other person knowing

Bad Faith Petitions-
When your ex files court documents based on false information or claims, just to keep you engaged in "law fare," legal harassment, depleting your money, resources and time

Badmouthing-
Someone saying negative comments about another person

Bag of Tricks-
The varied strategies that Abusers use to harm their Targets

Bait and Hook-
Where the Abuser deliberately provokes you so that you will react emotionally

Bait and Switch-
Abuser's strategy to win over the affection of their Target before they reveal their negative qualities

Baiting-
Abuser's tactic to intentionally provoke an emotional response from their Target, while they proclaim they are innocently unaware

Bandwagon Effect-
When a person aligns with the majority of others, even if their own opinion differs

Bankruptcy-
Legal proceeding when you are unable to pay your bills and debts

Bastard Child-
Offspring born out of wedlock and/or fatherless

Battered Spouse-
Spouse who is physically Abused and a Victim of Domestic Violence or Intimate Partner Terrorism

Batterer-
An Abuser who inflicts violent Physical Abuse on another

Battery-
The act of physically harming another

Battle Ground-
The fighting and adversarial scenario as a result of high conflict divorce

Behavior Therapy-
Psychotherapy that applies operant and classical conditioning to eliminate symptoms and environmental triggers of unhealthy behaviors without focusing on the psychological causes

Belittling-
Passive-aggressive, condescending behavior Abusers use to patronize or put down a Target while the Perpetrator is pretending to be friendly or reasonable

Betrayal-
The act of violating trust and confidence

Bidding-
The aligned people who support the Narcissist and gather information on their behalf

Bigamy-
When a married spouse is already married to someone else

Bipolar Disorder-
Formerly called Manic-Depression, is an illness that causes unusual up-and-down shifts in a person's mood, energy and behavior

Black and White Thinking-
When the Alienated Child(ren) believe one parent is All-Good and the other parent is All-Bad

Black Book-
A written detailed record of names from the Narcissist's various past, current and/or potential relationships with their contact information

Black Widow-
Female Narcissist who idealizes another and attracts them into her web of lies

Blackmail-
Abuser's actions to demand payment or compliance as a result of damaging or incriminating information that they have against the Victim

Blame Shifting-
Abusers turn the focus of responsibility on others because they don't take responsibility

Blaming-
Accusing someone else for being responsible for causing a problem instead of finding a way to deal with the issue

Blindsided-
Caught by surprise without warning

Blocked Access-
When your Alienating Abuser cuts off all means of communication of the Targeted Parent with their child(ren)

Boiling Frog Syndrome-
Abuser slowly causing pain to their Targets so they don't see the Abuse coming; just like a frog being slowly boiled in water is unaware that they are dying until it is too late

Boomerang Effect-
Reactance of the unintended consequences of efforts made to persuade another that comes back to hurt the originator

Borderline-
Personality Disordered Person who has trouble regulating their emotions

Boundaries-
The limits that you set to stay true to your values or protect yourself from Abusive others

Boundary Violations-
When someone does not respect your unwanted physical or emotional limits

Bottom Feeder-
An Abuser who uses other people's troubles and weaknesses as an opportunity

Brainwashing-
When the Abusing Alienator systematically uses mind control to force a False Narrative on you, your children or others

Breadcrumbing-
A Narcissist's attempts to send out false hope to a Target through flirting or cues without intention of a real commitment or desire for a sincere relationship

Broken Home-
A family that has experienced separation or divorce

Bullying-
Victimizing done by an Abuser which causes emotional distress and/or physical injury

Burnout-
When you are physically, emotionally or mentally exhausted as a result of dealing with an Abuser

Bystander-
Someone who sees Abuse or Alienation, but doesn't speak up or speak out

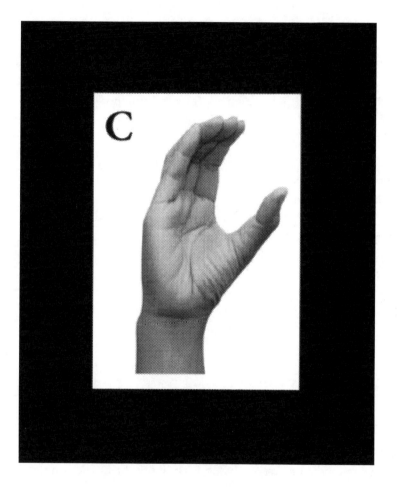

CPST-Complex Post Traumatic Stress Disorder-
Diagnosis when you experience repeated Trauma, Abuse or stress

Callousness-
When the Abuser is insensitive, indifferent and unsympathetic to the suffering of others

Campaign of Denigration-
Strong rejection of the loving, Targeted Parent even though the child(ren) experienced years of positive interactions and memories

Card Stacking-
Abuser's persuasion attempt to influence opinions through deliberate distortions, omission of information, overemphasizing false information and/or manipulating facts

Casual Sex-
When the Narcissist has sexual relations with a partner they don't know well

Catastrophizing-
Making a huge issue out of a small issue by assuming the worst

Catch and Release-
Hooking up with someone and letting them go without any commitment or becoming emotionally attached to them

Catfishing-
Luring someone into a relationship with lies and Fake Persona

Cerebral Narcissist-
An egocentric person who believes that they are superior, belittling and using their intelligence against others

Chameleon-
A person who changes their opinions or behavior according to the situation or who they are with

Chaos and Confusion-
A state of disorder or disbelief, often instigated by the Narcissist

Chaos Manufacture-
Creating or maintaining unnecessary risks, destruction or turmoil

Character Assassination-
Using malicious and unjustified means to harm a person's good reputation. Often done during the Abuser's Smear Campaign to get people against you so they can align with them

Charade-
A fraudulent person who claims to have a special knowledge or skill

Charlatan-
A fake and absurd show or pretense intended to portray a False Narrative

Cheater-
A person who has an affair or commits Adultery

Chemical Bond-
The brain's release of Dopamine and Oxytocin to create an addiction between Targets and their Abusers

Child Abuse-
Physical, emotional, sexual, neglect or harm to a child(ren) by their parent, guardian or other. Parental Alienation is considered an extreme form of Child Abuse

Child Advocacy-
Person or organization who intervenes on behalf of the well-being of children

Child Custody-
The care, protection and supervision of a child, determined by a court in divorce proceedings

Child Neglect-
When an Abusing Parent or Caregiver denies attention, care or affection considered essential for a child's wellbeing

Child Pornography-
Visual material which illegally sexualizes naked children or shows children participating in sexual acts. A common addiction of Covert Malignant Narcissists

Child Protective Services-CPS-
A governmental agency that is charged with responding to reports of Child Abuse or Neglect

Child Support-
Regular payments after a divorce or separation made by one parent to another to financially support the child(ren)

Child Welfare Agency-
Government organization with legal authorities which is charged with addressing the emotional and physical well-being of children

Childhood Amnesia-
The inability to recall events in early childhood due to Abuse, Trauma and/or Alienation

Childhood Trauma-
The negative experiences of a child that causes emotional or physical harm, resulting in lasting mental and physical effects

Choice Supply-
The Narcissist's number one/A relationship

Chosen Child-
The Child that the Abusing Parent or Alienator picks to shower the most attention on

Chosen Parent-
The Alienating Parent who the child(ren) align with despite that parent's Abuse and malevolence

Chronic Broken Promises-
When the Narcissist continually makes and then breaks commitments and vows

Chronic Trauma-
Abuse that happens over and over again

Circular Conversations-
Arguments that go on endlessly, repeating the same points and with no resolution

Classic Narcissist-
Diagnosis for a person who has an inability or unwillingness to recognize the needs and feelings of others, and is envious and acts in an arrogant and entitled way

Clinical Psychologist-
A licensed Mental Health professional who has an advanced degree and training in Psychology

Closet Narcissist-
A Covert or Vulnerable Narcissist who is introverted and shy

Closure-
The ending of a relationship with the Narcissist, however closure, as it is typically referred to, rarely happens with a Narcissist

Cloud Nine-
The feeling of being extremely happy

Cluster B Personality Disorder-
Diagnosis for people who are Antisocial, Borderline, Histrionic and/or Narcissistic

Coached to Lie-
When an Abuser, often an Alienating Parent, coerces a child not to tell the truth

Codependency-
When you have an unhealthy reliance on someone else

Coercion-
When the Abuser forces or attempts to force a Target to think or act against their will

Coercive Control-
Pattern of behavior used to intimidate and manipulate and punish you or others, which may include assault, threats, humiliation and/or intimidation

Coercive Snapshotting-
The Narcissist manipulating the Target by using introjection (the unconscious adoption of other's ideas or attitudes) on his/her partner and then idealizing the resultant internal object

Cognitive Behavioral Therapy-CBT
Talking therapy that helps you manage trauma and anxiety by changing the way you think and behave

Cognitive Dissonance-
Holding two or more contradictory beliefs, ideas and/or values

Cognitive Restructuring-
The process of changing the way you view a situation to change your emotional and behavioral response to it

Collapsed Narcissist-
A Narcissist who has experienced failure, humiliation or a blow to their fragile ego

Collateral Damage-
Injury to those innocent people left in the Narcissistic Abuser's or Alienator's wake

Collective Narcissism-
A group of people who together believe they are more superior than others

Collective Trauma-
Psychological reactions to Trauma that affects a group, such as a family

Combat Wounds-
The suffering and/or damage done to Victims and others as a result of Narcissistic Abuse or Domestic Violence

Communal Narcissist-
A person within a certain environment who has a grandiose, inflated perception of themself

Compartmentalization-
The ability to separate your thoughts and behaviors into distinct segments to manage and/or justify conflicting thoughts

Compassion Fatigue-
When the Target's emotional energy is depleted and they feel exhausted or hopeless

Competitive-
Aiming to be better than others. Narcissists are often very aggressive in vying situations, even with their own children

Complex PTSD-Complex Post Traumatic Stress Disorder-CPTSD-
Condition where someone has difficulty controlling their emotions after experiencing severe adversity and/or a traumatic event

Complex Trauma-
When a person, including a trusted caregiver, Abuses another, and the consequences continue long after the Abuse and/or Domestic Violence has ended

Compulsive Abuser-
When your partner obsesses over hurting you, and continues to engage in malevolent actions to inflict harm after the divorce or separation

Con-
A deceitful action or a person who persuades with deception

Condescending-
When someone puts you and/or your ideas down. Passive-aggressive behavior patronizing Abusers use to belittle or put down a Target while pretending to be friendly or reasonable

Conditional Love-
Love given by an Abusing, Alienating Parent or other, which is dependent on their child's or Target's loyalty and alignment

Conditioning-
The process of training or accustoming someone to behave in a certain way

Confession-
When someone admits to their wrongdoings

Confirmation Bias-
Paying more attention to viewpoints that reinforce your beliefs as opposed to a different take that you don't agree with

Confrontational-
When someone behaves with an aggressive, direct challenge

Confusion-
The uncertain state of being bewildered or unclear about something

Connect the Dots-
Figuring out that there is a relationship between certain behaviors or actions, leading to discovery

Contempt-
When the judge finds the respondent violated a provision of a court order. Unfortunately Abusers are rarely held in Contempt and Victims don't usually have the money or emotional strength to take their Abusers back to court because they violated a court order

Contempt of Court-
When your ex does not follow a court order

Contentious Divorce-
Legal separation with a spouse who disputes fair outcomes and makes things legally difficult for the other spouse

Contradictory Parenting-
When one parent's views, beliefs, rules, expectations and practices differ from the other parent's

Contrived Memories-
Remembering events that are distorted, fabricated or misinterpreted from reality

Control-
The power to influence people's perceptions, behavior, events or outcomes

Control-Me Syndrome-
Some Targets seek out relationships with those people who are Narcissistic and anti-social

Coparenting-
When both divorced or separated parents work together for the best interest of their child(ren)

Coping Mechanisms-
Strategies used to get through times of stress and manage painful emotions

Core Healing-
Addressing underlying symptoms such as depression, anxiety and low self-esteem, when coming to terms with issues and moving forward after experiencing Abuse or Trauma

Core Wounds-
Deep seated, underlying traumas that affect current issues and functioning

Counseling-
Therapy sessions to help understand issues and behaviors, and provide strategies to cope, heal and move forward

Counterdependency-
Behavior pattern where you avoid relying on someone to get support because of fear or lack of trust

Counterintuitive-
Something that feels wrong, against common sense or your intuition

Courage-
The ability to be strong in the face of fear, pain or grief

Court-
A tribunal presided over by a judge. The place to get legally divorced from your spouse. Also, the place where Abusers love to create chaos and force their Targets to spend a great deal of money defending the truth and what is morally right or equitable

Court Order-
A judgment or official proclamation based on a legal decision by a judge after a hearing

Covert-

Hiding behavior and being secretive. Narcissists' Abusive actions can be disguised under a cloak of care

Covert Narcissist-

Entitled person who feels superior, but pretends to be Empathetic, often going under the radar with their Abusive, calculating and malevolent behavior

Crazy Ex-

The name the Narcissist gives to his/her past spouses or partners, whether they behaved in a "crazy" manner or not, when in reality their ex is discerning and difficult for the Abuser to manipulate

Crazymaking-

Abuser's Gaslighting tactic to make his/her Target question reality as they experience self-doubt and confusion

Creeping-

A person who persistently follows someone, in person or online, in a stealth manner

Criminal Mind-

The thinking of someone who is immoral and/or breaks the law

Crocodile Tears-

Fake crying to elicit sympathy from others

Cross Generational Trauma-

Cumulative emotional and psychological wounding across generations

Cult-

Group where followers have a strong devotion to an Abusing leader who exploits and manipulates them

Cult Leader-
Abuser who demands loyalty and devoted obedience from others using deceptive means in order to exploit and manipulate; term used to describe the Favored, Alienating Parent

Custodial Interference-
When one parent intentionally gets in the way and creates obstacles with the other parent's child custody

Custodial Parent-
The parent who has physical custody of and lives full-time with the child(ren)

Custodial Plan-
A written outline of how the child(ren) will spend time with each parent

Custodial Rights-
A legal order as to how the parents will care for their child(ren)

Custody Battle-
Legal court proceedings to determine the percentage of time each parent will receive after divorce

Cutting Ties-
Breaking away from a relationship, including family members, due to Estrangement, Alienation, Abuse and/or protecting your emotional or physical safety

Cycle of Abuse-
The pattern of how Narcissists repeatedly Idealize, Devalue and Discard a Target or Victim

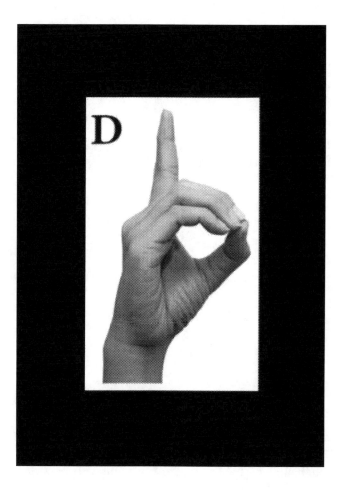

DARVO-Deny, Attack, and Reverse Victim and Offender-
A reaction of the Abuser when he/she is caught in their wrongdoing

DASH-Domestic Abuse, Stalking and Harassment-
A Risk Indicator Checklist (RIC) used to assess Victims of Domestic Abuse

DCFS-Department of Children and Family Services-
A governmental agency that is charged with responding to reports of Child Abuse or Neglect

Damage Control-
Actions taken to limit the harm caused by a person or situation

Damaged Goods-
A person who is no longer considered desirable or valuable to an Abuser

Dangling the Carrot-
Encouraging behavior by giving the impression of a desired outcome

Dark Empath-
A person who exploits their ability to understand how other people think and feel

Dark Knight-
A person that takes over another person with power and control

Dark Tetrad-
Four personality traits related to criminal and antisocial behavior that Abusers have due to their lack of Empathy and remorselessness and need to exploit and manipulate their Targets: Narcissism, Psychopathy, Machiavellianism and Sadism

Dark Triad-
Term that includes the three dangerous personality traits of Narcissism, Machiavellianism and Psychopathy

Dating-
Going out and getting to know another person you are considering for a romantic relationship

Deadbeat Parent-
A parent who is not there for or supports his/her child(ren)

Debt-
Something that is owed to someone else

Deceit-
Conscious effort to conceal the truth

Deception-
Abuser's distortion of and withholding the truth to mislead his/her Target

Deep Dive-
A hard look at something, often your own patterns and behaviors in relationships

Defamation-
Damaging the good reputation of someone by slander, libel or a Smear Campaign

Defending the Truth-
Arguing for your honest convictions

Defense Mechanism-
Unconscious reaction to protect yourself from anxious thoughts, uncomfortable actions or Abuse

Deflated Ego-
When your confidence and sense of self are diminished

Deflecting-
Changing the focus to something other than the real issue

Degradation-
Abuser's put downs to make his/her Target feel unworthy

Delayed Gratification-
Forgoing of immediate reward to string someone along

Delusional-
False and irrational belief not grounded in reality

Delusional Jealousy-
False belief that a spouse or partner is unfaithful

Denial-
Making excuses for or not taking ownership of one's behavior or the situation

Denied Custody-
Court not allowing a parent to share in the custodial care of their own child(ren)

Dependency-
Unhealthy reliance on someone else. A tactic used by a Parent Alienator to gain loyalty of their child(ren)

Dependent Personality Disorder-
Where someone is diagnosed with being excessively reliant on someone else

Depleted Resources-
When you have run out of and used up your money or support

Depression-
Negative and prolonged affective state of sadness and despondency

Deprogramming-
Strategy or process to restore values back from highly coercive and negative beliefs

Desertion-
When a person unilaterally decides to move out of the marital home

Detachment-
Separating yourself emotionally and physically from your Abuser

Detective-
The investigative role the Target ends up playing to uncover the truth about their Abuser's secrets

Devalue Phase-
When the Abuser stops caring for their Target, emotionally wounding them with verbal Abuse, withholding, humiliation and smearing

Developmental Trauma-
Experiencing, witnessing or chronic exposure to multitude of negative experiences, including: Abandonment, Betrayal, Physical or Sexual Assaults, Coercion and/or Emotional Abuse

Devoid of Empathy-
Someone that cannot feel other's emotions or pain

Dialectical Behavior Therapy-DBT-
Counseling that helps people accept the reality of their lives and make positive, healthy changes

Difficult Person-
Subjective description to describe multiple ways a relationship with an individual can be challenging, however Narcissists take that to the next level because their calculated actions are Abusive and psychologically damaging

Dimming Your Light-
Abuser's comments and actions to make the Target feel unworthy and not capable or special

Dirt Diving-
When the Narcissist has to get his/her supply from low places with people they don't value

Dirty Laundry-
Idiom when one person makes public their personal, private and/or embarracing matters or problems

Disarming the Narcissist-
Statements or actions that put the Narcissist in his/her place as unimportant

Discard-
When the Abuser suddenly cuts you off or breaks up. Targeted Victims can also muster up the courage to escape from and leave their Abuser

Disconnect-
Dissociate, step away or tune out from a person or situation

Discovery-
The detailed exchange of financials and information in a divorce or court proceeding. The Narcissists often lie, hide assets, over-inflate debts and provide misrepresented facts and figures

Disengaging-
Withdrawing from a person or situation

Dishonesty-
Not telling the truth

Dismissive-
Ignoring, feeling or showing that something or someone is unworthy or insignificant

Disneyland/Disneyworld Parent-
Parent who just shows up with presents, money or trips and doesn't stay around for or care about their child's feelings or everyday issues or events

Disparage-
The put down of another person

Displacement-
When an Abuser shifts impulses to mistreat one Target to a less threatening Target

Disruptive Attachment-
When a child's bond with the parent(s) is interrupted, causing a wide range of insecurities and behaviors

Dissimilar Replacement-
When the Narcissist seeks a new supply who is extremely different than the Target in most every way, including choosing a new partner of different ethnic and cultural origin. This is common with Narcissistic Mortification

Dissociation-
Feeling disconnected to the reality of the Abuse that is happening to you

Dissociative Collapse-
Losing your sense of self due to extreme trauma

Dissociative Disorder-
Disruption of a person's consciousness, memory or perceptions

Dissolution-
Another word for divorce, or the falling apart of a relationship

Distorted Reality-
Inaccurate perception of a situation

Diversion Tactics-
Strategies to deflect responsibility used by Narcissists to exploit and Abuse, such as Gaslighting, Blame Shifting, Word Salad, Threats, Projection, Love Bombing and/or Triangulation

Divide and Conquer-
When the Abuser isolates and manipulates you or others to gain control

Divorce-
Legal dissolution of and separation from marriage

Divorce Decree-
Final judgment in a divorce, however those who have divorced an Abusing Narcissist know that it is not always over when it's supposed to be over, as Abusers misuse the legal system to stalk, harass and obsess over the destruction of their ex

Divorce Drama-
The theatrics one person will engage in while in divorce proceedings

Dog Whistling-
Baiting tactic used in front of others to humiliate their Target

Domestic Abuse-
Abuser's pattern of coercive behaviors to exert power and control over their familial Target

Domestic Abuse Advocate-
A professional who provides resources and/or helps a Victim stand up for themselves

Domestic Abuse Shelter-
A temporary place to live if you are escaping harm from your spouse

Domestic Family Terrorism-
An Abusive act to a person within the family who is physically or emotionally harmed and a Victim of Violence

Domestic Terrorist-
A person within the family who physically or emotionally abuses another through Domestic Violence or Intimate Partner Terrorism

Domestic Theft-
When your ex steals money, assets, resources and even the marital home without asking

Domestic Violence-
Physical or Emotional Abuse within the home or within a familial relationship

Domestic Violence Wheel-
A circle chart for advocates and Victims to identify patterns of Abusive behaviors

Domineering-
Asserting one's will and power over another in a rude and controlling way

Doormat-
A submissive person who allows others to dominate them

Dosing-
Abuser's giving of small bits of positive attention to their Targets after being cruel, to keep them strung along

Double Bind-
A situation where there are two or more contradictory messages or outcomes

Double Life-
When your spouse is carrying on a relationship or has a family with someone else

Double Standards-
Abuser's two sets of rules: high standards of honesty and fidelity for the Target, but not for themselves. Rules for thee, but not for me

Double Talk-
Saying one thing, while also contradicting themselves and saying another thing

<u>Drama-</u>
Making a simple situation into an attention-drawing, theatrical event

<u>Drama Triangle-</u>
Destructive interactions in conflict between the Victim, Persecutor and Rescuer

<u>Dual Identity-</u>
Survival mechanism of Splitting, where the Abused person takes on two different personas (authentic self vs. false self) to avoid further Abuse

<u>Duping Delight-</u>
Abuser's compulsive habit of pathologically lying for control and enjoyment

<u>Dysfunctional Family-</u>
Impaired, toxic or Abusive relationships with immediate relatives

<u>Dysfunctional Relationship-</u>
Impaired, toxic or Abusive interactions with a friend, acquaintance, partner or spouse

Echo-
A nymph in Greek mythology who could not tempt Narcissus, a figure who believed himself to be so handsome he fell in love with his own refection

Echoism-
The opposite of Narcissism, where a person unselfishly feels the need to take care of others at their own expense and detriment

Education-
Doing the work to research, understand and learn about Domestic Violence, Narcissistic Abuse, Parental Alienation and Intergenerational Family Trauma

Ego-
The self, your personality and perceptions. Ego is inflated in Narcissists

Ego-Syntonic/Dystonic-
When a disorder produces behaviors related to a person's self-image

Egofrugality-
Inflated sense of self and fragile ego resulting from self-doubt, insecurity and lack of self-esteem as a result of Abuse, neglect or trauma

Emotional Abuse-
Verbal attacks using criticism, humiliation, Gaslighting, Smearing, Devaluing and intimidation

Emotional Baggage-
The negative feelings you have about your past and the Trauma that you've experienced

Emotional Blackmail-
Manipulation where an Abuser will use your feelings to control your behavior so they get what they want

Emotional Cut Off-
Choosing to stop the interpersonal attachment with another

Emotional Damage-
Hurt caused by the non-physical disparaging from an Abuser

Emotional Dysregulation-
Your negative response that seems extreme for the situation

Emotional Elevator-
Experiencing the ups and down of feelings, with varying levels of emotions

Emotional Hijacking-
Where our mental thoughts interfere with our ability to make good decisions

Emotional Incest-
Non-physical Sexual Abuse between a parent and child

Emotional Neglect-
When someone's needs are consistently disregarded, ignored, unappreciated and/or invalidated

Emotional Regulation-
The ability to reasonably manage your thoughts and feelings

Emotional Trigger-
A reminder that evokes strong feelings and stress

Emotional Unavailability-
When the Narcissist is unable or unwilling to be emotionally intimate with a Target

Emotional Vampire-
A person who sucks and drains your emotional energy

Emotionally Bankrupt-
When the Target focuses so much on the Abuser that they become wiped out

Empath-
A person who deeply understands the feelings of others

Empathy-
When an intuitive person identifies with or experiences the thoughts and feelings of another

Empowerment-
Gaining the confidence and skills necessary to move forward after experiencing Adversity

Empty Promises-
Unfulfilled commitments and vows that lack real substance or intent. Narcissists Future Fake with Empty Promises during the Love Bomb phase

Enabler-
Supportive person who consciously or unconsciously allows negative behavior to continue

Energy Vampires-
A person who sucks and drains your energy, stamina, time, thoughts and feelings

Enforce Court Orders-
When you have to go to court to get an authority to order your ex follow legal/court decisions

Engulfment-
Unhealthy and overwhelming dependency and attention on someone else because they feel unworthy otherwise

Enlisting Supporters-
The Narcissist's Flying Monkeys who are recruited to align with them based on a False Narrative

Enmeshment-
When your relationship with someone is characterized by unhealthy Boundaries, Codependency, being overly close and symbiotic, where there is a loss of individuality, autonomy, critical reasoning skills and a sense of self

Entitlement-
Abuser's belief that they are superior, unique and deserve special treatment

Envy-
When the Narcissist strongly desires to possess something another person has, such as money, assets and success

Erased Family-
When an Alienated Child unjustly cuts off the Targeted Parent's side of the family

Erased Parent-
The Targeted, loving, normal-range parent who is Alienated from his/her child(ren)

Eroded Identity-
When your confidence and belief about yourself is questioned by Gaslighting

Erratic Behavior-
Inconsistent and unpredictable actions that are illogical, extreme or unrelated for the situation

Escape Plan-
A set of steps to safely remove yourself from your Abuser

Estranged Children-
When your kids decide to separate or distance themselves from a parent or family. Usually this is done to protect themselves from Abuse or Harm. Not to be confused with Alienation, which is done by Coercive Control and the influence of the other parent

Estrangement-
When a person makes the choice to physically distance themselves from another because of their negative thoughts, feelings or harmful experiences

Ethos-
Integrity and character. Empaths live with high level ethos and their actions speak louder than words, whereas Narcissists don't live with high level ethos, but have the need to tell people they do

Evil Enemy-
Your Abusive ex or how your ex sees you after you file for divorce

Evil Eye-
A gaze or look of hostility and disapproval

Evildoer-
Person who commits profoundly immoral, evil and malevolent deeds

Ex-
Your former spouse or partner

Ex Recycling-
When the Narcissist returns to former partners for attention and control

Exchanging the Children-
Court-ordered time to switch care of child(ren) for their parenting time

Exhibitionist Narcissist-
Bragging Narcissists who need to be publicly admired for their success

Existential Loneliness-
Deep sense of isolation and disconnection with others due to the forced and covert separation of your support system by the Abuser

Exit Strategy-
A plan to safely escape from your Abuser

Expert-
A professional who is qualified to give substantiated testimony

Exploitation-
Treating someone unfairly to benefit from their work or character

Explosive Sadism-
Unpredictable and furious outbursts with uncontrollable rage and fearsome attacks

Exposing the Narcissist-
When the Abuser's secrets or malevolent behavior is revealed publicly. Being Exposed is one of the Narcissist's biggest fears

External Solution-
The Narcissist's persecutory justification for the Target discarding them first, before they get a chance to do it, is that the Target is evil, bad or malicious. The only way the Narcissist can accept that the Target left them first is to Smear the Target's good name and character, and share with others how (falsely) awful their ex was

External Validation-
When someone needs another person's recognition to feel worthy

Extortion-
Abuser's efforts of obtaining something, especially money, through force, threats and intimidation

Extramarital Affair-
Cheating on your spouse, infidelity

Extreme Parental Alienation-
Where the Abusing Alienating Parent intentionally displays to the child unjustified negativity about their other loving parent to turn them against them with hatred, fear, implanted memories and lies so the child(ren) will align with the Alienator and their False Narrative

Extrinsically Motivated-
Tangible incentives to encourage behavior, with punishments and rewards

Extroverted Narcissist-
Self-absorbed individual who puts energy into outward appearances, people and things, rather than inward influences

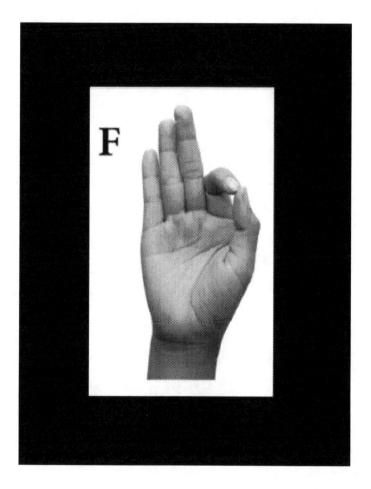

FOG-Fear, Obligation and Guilt-
Tactics Abusers use to control and threaten their Targets and keep them in a haze to doubt their own judgment

Fabrications-
The act of concocting or inventing information or stories with the intent to deceive

Facade-
The outward appearance that Narcissistic Abusers and Alienators portray to conceal their true, malevolent behavior

Factitious Disorder-
Child Abusing Mental Illness where a parent makes up false symptoms for attention and to make their child look sick. Sometimes referred to as Munchausen Syndrome by Proxy

Factor One Psychopathy-
The measurement of the Narcissistic Abuser's selfish, remorseless and exploitative use of others

Fairytale-
The belief that your relationship, marriage or family is ideal and extremely happy

Fake Empathy-
Abusers pretending to care about their Targets

Fake Intimacy-
Abuser's pretending to be attracted to a Target

False Accusations-
Abuser's blaming their Target for something they didn't do. Often False Accusations are a projection to accuse someone else of what the Abuser has done

False Arrest-
When law authorities charge and take an innocent Target into custody, based on untrue claims from an Abuser who is out to destroy their Target in every way

False Beliefs-
Misconception from incorrect reasoning based on un-truths

False Flattery-
Love-Bombing tactic of fake compliments to their Target to get them to return compliments back

False Friends-
People you thought cared for you, but don't. They may act kind to your face, but have malevolent intentions

False Hopes-
When you are looking forward to something, but eventually you learn that the Narcissist has Future Faked or made empty promises, even though he/she had no intention of following through

False Image-
How the Narcissists incorrectly sees themselves

False Mask-
The Fake Public Persona displayed by the Narcissist to cover up who they really are

False Narrative-
Abuser's untrue story about his/her Target to gain support, smear their ex and change people's positive perceptions to negative

False Persona-
Abusers fool others with an inaccurate belief of who they really are. It's referred to wearing a mask to hide their inadequacies and covert, malevolent behavior

Falsify Documents-
Intentionally manipulating numbers and making dishonest statements on paperwork. Narcissists are masters of creating professional looking spreadsheets with inaccurate numbers

Familicide-
The murder or murder-suicide where someone kills multiple close family members, and sometimes themselves

Family Court-
A tribunal presided over by a judge. The place to get legally divorced from your spouse. Also, the place where Abusers love to create chaos and force their honest Targets to spend a great deal of money defending the truth and what is morally right and fair. Unfortunately, truth, equity and justice does not always prevail in Family Court when an honest, Targeted person has to defend themselves against a conniving, manipulative and deceitful Narcissist

Family Estrangement-
When a person makes the choice to physically distance themselves from their some members or the entire family because of their negative thoughts, feelings or harmful experiences

Family of Origin-
The family (either biological or not) in which someone was raised

Family Secrets-
Information that is taboo and not shared with those outside of the family

Family Therapy-
Treatment of parents and child(ren) that focuses on analyzing problems and conflict and using techniques or discussion to change the negative issues or patterns with contracts, instruction, modeling and rehearsal

Fantasy-
Narcissist's false beliefs of grandiosity, success and heroism

Father Wounds-
The long-term consequences when a dad is absentee or has been emotionally distant or Abusive

Faulty Programming-
Deliberate, calculated, focused, repeated and misguided mind control to instill and reinforce someone's behavior or ideas

Fauxpology-
When the Abuser gives you a fake or insincere apology with no remorse

Favored Parent-
The preferred parent with whom a child(ren) has aligned with; that parent is usually the Child Abusing Alienator who turns the child(ren) against the normal-range Loving Parent

Favoritism-
Systematically giving preferential treatment to one person as opposed to equal treatment for all

Fawn Response-
When empathetic Targets abandon their own needs to serve others to avoid conflict or disapproval

Fear-
Being afraid of your Abuser, especially if you don't comply with their desires or demands

Fearmongering-
When your Abuser deliberately instills fear to traumatize you

Fight or Flight-
Sympathetic nervous system response, with an increased rush of adrenaline, to threatening or stressful situations, leading to altering your physical and emotional responses

Filicide-
The extreme action when the Abusive ex kills the child(ren) so the Targeted Parent suffers the ultimate Parental Alienation

Filings-
Legal petitions against you, your spouse or partner

Final Discard-
When the Narcissist leaves for good, and breaks up in a very mean and painful way, however they usually return in a Hoover attempt

Financial Abuse-
When your Abusing intimate partner controls access to all money, bills, bank accounts, investments, spending, etc. limiting the Victim's capacity to support themselves so they are dependent on their Abuser

Financial Affidavit-
Statement showing income, expenses, debts and assets; a form with numbers that can is often altered by a Financial Abuser who will inflate debts and deflate assets

Flashbacks-
Remembering and reliving Traumatic experiences after a Triggering event. Associated with Post Traumatic Stress Disorder

Flirtatious Behavior-
Social and/or sexual actions, body language or words, used to tease or suggest interest in a deeper relationship with another

Fluffing-
Strategy for Targets to use with Narcissists where you flatter them to poof up their ego so you can get through a situation

Flying Monkeys-
People who believe and align with your Abuser and do the dirty work bidding and gathering of information for them; term taken from the Flying Monkeys who served the Wicked Witch in the Wizard of Oz

Fog Lifting-
The feeling of being able to think more clearly about your unhealthy relationship with the Narcissist

Forced Marriage-
Arranged marital union where one or both parties do not give their consent

Forensic Professional-
An expert hired to investigate the covert actions of your ex Secret Agent spouse

Foster Care-
Temporary living arrangement coordinated by the government for children who have been removed from their parents

Fractured Family-
Broken family due to divorce, Estrangement and Parental Alienation

Fragile Ego-
Inflated sense of self resulting from self-doubt, insecurity and lack of self-esteem as a result of Abuse, neglect or trauma

Fragmented Child-
The psychological Splitting of your child's ego due to Parental Alienation

Free Range Parenting-
Parents who are extremely permissive and uninvolved, allowing natural consequences to result from the kids' behavior

Frenemy-
Someone who poses as your friend, but is really an enemy

Frivolous Litigation-
When your Abuser misuses the judicial system to hurt, harass, deplete your money in fees and gain economic advantage over minute issues using false allegations

Fuel-

The Abuser's Narcissistic Supply and constant need to fulfill their self-esteem needs and emptiness within them with people who provide attention, adoration and support

Functional Amnesia-

The memory loss due to the Trauma you have experienced

Future Faking-

Abuser's manipulative tactic to make future promises that will never be kept and grandiose life plans that will never materialize, just to keep stringing their Victim or Target along

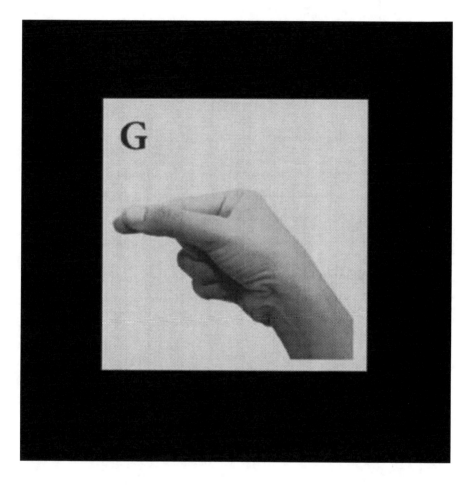

Gag Order-
Mum Clause that legally prevents the Target from speaking the truth in public

Gangstalking-
When you are being followed, stalked and harassed by many people

Garden Variety Narcissist-
Narcissists who try to get others to please them or take care of them

Gaslighting-
Abusive tactic used to make you doubt yourself and your sanity by systematically undermining your thoughts or abilities by providing conflicting, untruthful information. Term from the 1944 movie "Gaslight" where the Narcissistic husband manipulates things to make his wife feel like she is going crazy and questions herself and reality

Gatekeeper Parent-
When the attitudes, behavior or legal petitions of the Abusive, Alienating ex limits the Targeted Parent's access, contact or involvement with the child(ren)

Generalized Anxiety Disorder-GAD-
Excessive stress about a wide range of concerns accompanied by physical and emotional symptoms

Generational Abuse-
Cumulative emotional and psychological wounding across generations within a family

Gett Refusal-
When your Jewish husband refuses to grant you a divorce

Ghosted-
Being suddenly cut off from all communication without explanation

Gigalo-
A man who depends on a women to support him financially, like a male prostitute

Going No Contact-
Stopping all forms of communication and cutting ties between the Abuser and the Target

Golden Child-
The favorite child excessively praised for achievements, who is viewed as an extension of the Narcissist, so they lose their individual identity

Good Enough Parent-
A dad or mom who cares for his/her child in any way that is adequate for proper development

Gossip-
Badmouthing, negative talk or rumors about the personal business of others

Grand Slam-
When the Narcissist experiences a sweeping success or total victory

Grandiose Narcissist-
An assertive, extroverted Narcissist with high self-esteem, entitlement, over-confidence, sense of superiority and a willingness to exploit others

Grandiosity-
Person who has delusions of grandeur, entitlement, arrogance and exaggerated self-importance

Grandstanding-
Behaving in a showy or ostentatious manner in an attempt to attract a Target

Grey Rock-
Communication and boundary-setting technique where you give a boring or non-reactive response to limit your Abuse

Grief-
Experiencing anguish and severe sadness after significant loss. Targeted parents grieve the death of their living Alienated child(ren)

Grooming-
When the Abuser shapes the narrative and sets up the Target for Abuse, slowly mixing both positive and negative behavior for exploitation

Guardian Ad Litem-GAL-
A court-appointed representative who is charged with intervening in legal Child Custody recommendations

Guilt Tripping-
Emotional manipulation to make someone feel bad or responsible for what they said or did

Gut Intuition-
Your instinctual, immediate inner feeling about something or someone

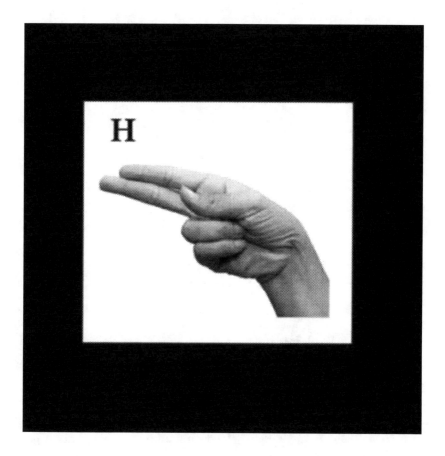

Halo Effect-
When someone judges another as more intelligent, competent or honest than he/she actually is

Hamster Wheel-
Being busy all the time, but not achieving your goals

Harassment-
When an Abuser insults, stalks or harms their Target with ongoing torment and bullying

Harem-
Collection of admirers who are in line to provide Supply to the egotistical Narcissist

Harem Closet/Garage-
The group of people on the sidelines, ready to supply attention to the Narcissist

Harem Scrolling-
When the Narcissist is going through his/her list of people to connect with

Hate-
Hostile emotion with intense feelings of anger and detestation with a desire to inflict pain and misery. Alienators hate their ex more than they love their children

Haughtiness-
Narcissist's behavior and self belief coming across as arrogant, superior and above others

Healed Empath-
Learning to understand the positive personality trait of feeling other's emotions and managing it with the negative consequences of being an Empath

Healing Journey-
The process of going from experiencing Abuse and suffering to finding resources, researching and connecting with others to be self-actualized and more at peace

Healing Process-
Recovering and surviving after experiencing Abuse, harm and/or trauma

Healthy Boundaries-
Actions in relationships that draw a line on what behavior is acceptable and what is not

Heartache-
Deep emotional anguish or grief caused by the loss or absence of someone

Hedonism-
The Narcissist's constant pursuit of pleasure and sensual self-indulgence

Helicopter Parent-
A parent who is overprotective and controlling or shows an excessive interest in their child(ren)

Hero-
A person who is admired or idealized for courage, outstanding achievements or noble qualities

Hidden Abuse-
Covert mistreatment that is not easily recognized by outsiders

Hidden Assets-
When your spouse or ex has accounts, money, investments, legal documents and/or material possessions that are kept secret from the other spouse

High Conflict Divorce-
Divorces where one or both parties engage in extremely adversarial and negative behavior to intentionally interfere with the legal process of ending the marriage

High Conflict Personality-
A person who consistently acts in a way that intensifies or prolongs adversarial interactions with others

Highly Sensitive Person-
An empathetic individual who has a heightened awareness of others' feelings and the stimuli around them

Hijacked Mind-
When Abusers manipulate the emotions and thoughts of others; this Brainwashing is a common experience with Alienated Children

Historical Trauma-
Cumulative emotional and psychological wounding across generations

Histrionic Personality Disorder-
Pattern of long-term (not episodic) self-dramatization by someone who craves attention and overreacts to minor events. They are manipulative, egocentric, demanding and dependent

Holidays Ruined-
Typical holiday scenario for Narcissists is to interfere with celebrations because of their insatiable need for attention. Abusers want to lower their Target's expectations for happiness

Holographic Projection-
The Narcissist's ability to present a positive, charming or desirable public image, while being a negative, manipulative Abuser

Honor Based Violence-HBV-
Abuse carried out and justified to enforce rules related to cultural beliefs

Hooking Up-
Sexual encounters with no commitment or expectations

Hoop Jumping-
The Abuser's need to make their Targets do a number of things in order to please them

Hoovering-
When an Abuser tries to suck you back into the relationship after being Discarded

Hornet's Nest-
A situation fraught with extreme difficulty and complications. Narcissistic ex-spouses create this complicated chaos in their post-divorce legal petitions

Hostile Parenting-
When a parent regularly harms the child(ren) by shouting, physically Abusing, isolating, emotionally berating or disciplining in a way that effects the child's self-esteem

Humiliation-
Feelings of shame after being disgraced or deprecated

Hump and Dump-
When the Narcissist has sex with someone and then breaks up with them

Hurt and Rescue Cycle-
The cyclical pattern of when the Abuser causes harm to their Target and then helps the Victim out

Hurt People-Hurt People-
A rationale or excuse to explain why Narcissists Abuse others because they have previously endured Abuse, rather than putting the focus on their unacceptable behavior

Hyper Vigilance-
Heightened awareness and sensitivity to perceived threats

Hypocrisy-
Double-standard used by Narcissists to ignore their own shortfalls and project their demands onto others to avoid accountability

Hysteria-
Extreme overreaction to events and issues

Idealization Phase-
Early on when the Abuser admires and puts their Target on a pedestal, showering them with excessive praise and attention

Identity Erosion-
The Targets' slow loss of their ego and who they are due to Abuse

Identity Theft-
Abusers taking on someone else's sense of self or credentials

Ignored Red Flags-
When you don't pay attention to the signs that you are in an Abusive Relationship with a Narcissist

Illegitimate Child-
Offspring born out of wedlock

Implanted Memories-
Recollection of events that never happened but were convinced happened by someone else. Alienators will implant false memories to get their children to cut off the other parent

Imposter Syndrome-
Personality pattern characterized by pathological lying and fabricating their identity to gain recognition and status

Impulsive Borderline Personality Disorder-
Diagnosed condition characterized by impulsivity and temptations to harm

Impulsivity-
Reactive behavior with little or no thought, reflection or consideration of the consequences

Independent Thinker Phenomenon-
Alienated children's claim that their cutting off all communications with their loving, Targeted Parent is by their own choice and insist that they are not influenced by the Favored, Alienating parent

Indiscretions-
Behavior that lacks good judgment or refers to the Narcissist's secret rendezvous

Individual Safety Plan-ISP-
Personalized checklist to help a Victim prepare for their next Violent interaction with their Abuser

Indoctrination-
The Abuser, using his/her power and authority, attempts to systematically mold others' beliefs

Induced Conversation-
When the Narcissist transfers their malevolent, underhanded and negative emotions into you without any type of repercussion. These manipulating Abusers want their Targets to turn against themselves

Infantilization-
When Alienators encourage childish behavior in more Adult Children

Inferiority Complex-
Feelings of inadequacy and insecurity

Infidelity-
When a spouse or intimate partner cheats, becoming sexually or emotionally involved with another person

Inflated Ego-
Narcissist's distorted view of themselves, believing that they are superior when compared to others, are more worthy or more intelligent than they really are

Injustice-
Lack of fairness or reasonable results in court settlements with an Abuser

Inner Bonding-
Self-healing and self-love process of taking responsibility and ownership for feelings resulting from healing on many levels, including physically, emotionally and spiritually

Inner Child-
The connection you have with yourself to your early childhood memories and experiences

Inner Critic-
Criticism of yourself and your abilities; heightened after being Gaslit

Inner Peace-
Deep sense of calm and well-being

Inner Reflection-
The ability to search within and give serious thought about your own character, actions and motives

Insecure Attachment-
Negative parent-child relationship where child(ren) lacks confidence and is ambivalent and can be anxious or avoidant

Insecurity-
Feelings of inadequacy, lack of self-confidence and inability to cope

Integrity-
Staying true to your moral values of honesty, compassion and goodness

Intended Target-
The Victim who the Abuser is intentionally aiming to engage with

Intergenerational Abuse/Trauma-
When you realize the patterns of the adverse emotions and behaviors you are experiencing are similar to or caused by your family and descendants patterns

Intergenerational Family Trauma-
Cumulative emotional and psychological wounding across generations within a family

Interject-
Internal object or voice that the Narcissist uses to represent his/her Target, especially if the Targeted ex discarded them first

Intermittent Reinforcement-
Tactic and pattern of the Abuser randomly interspersing kindness between acts of cruelty, to keep the Target tied to the relationship

Internal Solution-
When the Narcissist, in his/ her grandiose defense, reframes the situation and takes credit for the discard, even when the Target was the one to escape and break off the relationship

Internal Validation-
When your own sense of self provides the worthiness you need

Intimacy Avoidance-
When a person is anxious about having an extremely close physical or emotional connection

Intimate Partner Violence-
Abuser who physically or emotionally Abuses their spouse or partner. Parental Alienation is considered by researchers to be an extreme form of Intimate Partner Violence

Intimate Terrorism-
A person who is physically or emotionally abused and a Victim of Domestic Violence at the hands of someone who is close to them

Intimidation-
When the Abuser exerts their power and control by using threats to cause fear in his/her Target

Intrinsically Motivated-
Acting for inherent satisfaction rather than appearances or external rewards

Introject-
How the Narcissist views others as objects or things to be used and Abused, as opposed to separate individuals with their own needs, thoughts, feelings and/or identities

Introverted Narcissist-
Covert, self-obsessed, manipulating Narcissist who lacks confidence

Intuition-
Your immediate insight from your gut feelings

Invalidation-
The process of denying, rejecting or dismissing someone else's feelings

Inverted Narcissist-
A manipulative and often charismatic Narcissist who was raised by a Narcissistic parent, and is an expert at people-pleasing

Invisible Child-
A child who doesn't stand out, follows the rules, isn't overly talented and doesn't draw attention to themselves

Isolation-
A manipulative strategy when the Abuser separates the Target from friends and family

Isomorphic Replacement-
When the Narcissist seeks new supply who has many of the same physical, emotional and cultural characteristics of the Target, their ex who escaped. This is common with Narcissistic Injury

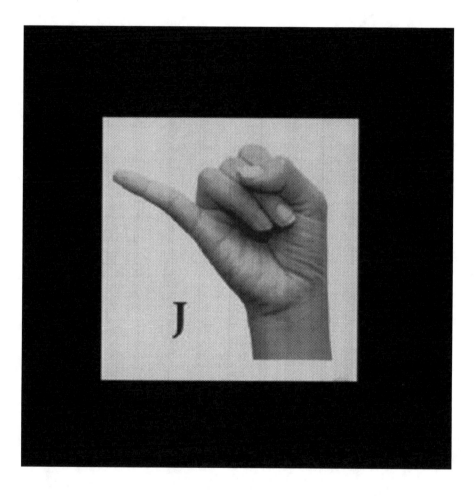

Jackknifed-
When an Abuser is going along and then switches tactics or behavior without warning

Jealousy-
Negative emotion of envy because your spouse or partner flirts with others and is interested in or is involved with someone else

Jekyll and Hyde-
Two different, opposing personalities and behaviors in one person

Jezebel Spirited-
Someone who is demonic and evil

Joint Custody-
When both parents share custody of their child(ren)

Journey-
Living life, experiencing the ups and downs over time and moving forward, leading to growth

Judging Ourselves-
The often negative narrative we use to define who we are after experiencing Abuse

Judgment-
The "final" divorce decree, although things are rarely "final" with Abusing Narcissists

Juggling Supply-
When the Narcissist interacts with multiple romantic partners at one time, doing their best to keep track of them all; Some Narcissists must keep a Little Black Book or make notes to identify or remember the details of the various people

Jump Effect-
The Narcissist's desire for intimacy or sex

Justice-
Fair and equitable outcome to court proceedings, which rarely happens for the Targeted, Abused spouse when divorcing an Abusing Narcissist

Kangaroo Court-
An idiom describing the disregarding of fair laws, procedures and justice. Targeted people often find that the Abuser's are not held legally accountable for perjury and falsified documents and that the settlements are often in the Abuser's favor and against the honest Victim

Karma-
Universal law of cause and effect. The belief that the energies you put out in the universe you will receive back at some point

Kernel of Truth-
Half-Lies told by Narcissists to get others to believe that they are honest, when they are not

Kidnapping-
Criminal offense of unlawfully abducting a child against their will or the other parent's will

Kobayashi Maru-
When the Target is in a No-Win situation

Lack of Conscience-
When an Abuser only cares about their own agenda and ignores morality and the feelings of others

Lack of Empathy-
Also called Apathy and is the inability to consider the emotional state of others. Classic characteristic of Narcissists

Lack of Remorse-
The inability of the Abuser to feel bad about the cruel and terrible things they do to hurt others

Landmines-
When the Abuser hides their anger and Abuse under the radar until he/she explodes with Narcissistic Rage

Lather, Rinse, Repeat-
Idiom for the cycle of repeated behaviors displayed by Abusing Narcissists

Lawfare-
When the Abuser uses the legal system to damage or delegitimize his/her Target with perjury, inaccurate figures and frivolous lawsuits/petitions, depleting the Target's energy, time and resources

Learned Helplessness-
The belief that you can't change or improve your circumstances

Legal Abduction-
Kidnapping of your child(ren) by the Abuser without breaking the law

Legal Abuse/Harassment-
When Abusers misuse the courts and file bad-faith petitions to cause personal stress and financial harm to their ex and keep them in litigation, depleting their money for legal fees and monopolizing their time

Letting Go-
Discontinuing the struggle and energy put forth with people and situations you cannot control

Leveling-
When the Narcissist reminds you of every bad thing that the Target has ever done to bring you down and make you weak and insecure

Liar-
A dishonest person

Libel-
Crime of making a false written statement that damages and defames a person's reputation

Life Lessons-
The trials, tribulations and experiences we must endure in order to grow and self-actualize

Lightbulb Moment-
When you suddenly realize what is going on and that you are a Victim of Abuse

Limerence-
Temporary psychological state of obsessive lust and intense infatuation of another with an overwhelming desire for romantic reciprocation, common with Victims of Narcissistic Abuse, as they are seeking attachment and attention after experiencing CPTSD and Trauma Bonding

Linen Cupboard-
Metaphor that explains how our awakened senses can open up very vivid and detailed memories

Lion's Den-
A place or situation where you must deal with an angry person or group of people

Litigation-
The process of arguing both sides in court

Loneliness-
The empty feeling of being solo or that no one wants to spend time with you

Lost Child-
The child who isolates themselves and retreats from family dysfunction because they feel overwhelmed

Love-
Complex emotion of strong feelings of affection and devotion

Love Bombed-
Abuser's over-the-top manipulation with an overload of attention with excessive admiration to seduce their Target

Love Child-
Offspring resulting from an affair

Love Withdrawal-
When the Alienating Parent takes away affection from their child if they say anything positive about the other parent

Low Contact-
Self-preserving strategy of being selective about how much you interact with someone, reserving communication for emergencies or holidays

Low Self Esteem-
Feeling bad about who you are and judging yourself negatively. Common symptom of Narcissistic Abuse and Gaslighting

Lucifer Effect-
Social situations that negatively influence and demonically corrupt a person's behavior in an evil way

Lucky Charm-

Someone who is very special and brings good fortune to another person

Lying By Omission-

Not telling the whole truth by leaving out important information, which fosters a misconception

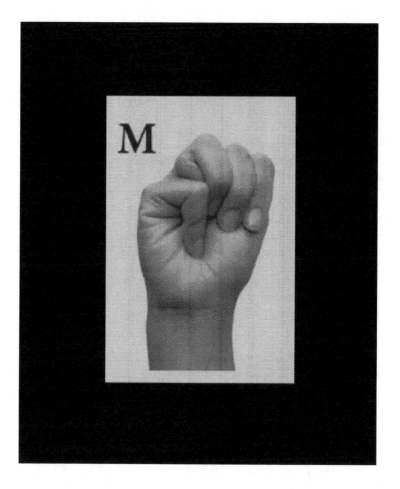

Machiavellianism-
Manipulative and exploitative behavior of Abuser who has a lack of Morals or Empathy

Magical Thinking-
The belief that the negative behavior of your Abuser can be influenced by the Target's positive thoughts and wishes

Maintenance-
Another name for marital alimony given to one spouse after a divorce

Malevolence-
Abuser's unfair, harsh and calculated treatment of their Target, whom they see as the enemy

Malevolent Narcissist-
A covert and calculating Abuser who harms others to gain attention, feed their sense of superiority or manipulate others and situations for their own benefit

Malicious Parent-
An Abusing Parent who shows vengeful behavior by deliberately engaging in Parental Alienation to sever the relationship between the child(ren) and the normal-range, Loving Targeted Parent

Malignant Narcissist-
Dangerous Abusing Psychopath who manipulates and aggressively exploits their Targets

Mandated Reporter-
Professional who is required to report suspicion of Abuse

Maneater-
A dominant woman who has many sexual partners

Manifest-
To make something happen by your thoughts, actions and intentions

Manipulation-
The use of various tactics to control you or the situation

Manufactured Emotions-
The fake feelings made up by the Narcissist to hook empathetic people in

Manufactured Lies-
Making up false statements in order to deceive others

Marginalized-
When the Target is treated as insignificant or peripheral

Marriage Vows-
A solemn promise made by two people who wed. Later you sometimes find out that only one of you honored your vows

Martyr-
An Abuser who tries to get sympathy from others, even though they are the one that caused the problem

Mascot Child-
A child who lessens the family anxiety by using distractions, deflections and/or humor

Mask-
The disguising of emotions and the Narcissist's true personality to deceive those around them into believing they are honest, genuine and upstanding

Mask Slipping-
Abuser's False Persona to hide their true, malevolent character being unintentionally revealed

Massaging-
The Abuser's constant manipulation of their Target to try to get what they want

Matriarch-
The domineering and powerful woman who is the head of the family

Mean and Sweet Cycle-
Abuser's pattern and strategy to win over the affection of their Target before they reveal their negative qualities

Mediation-
Impartial counseling to resolve issues in separation or divorce

Megalomaniac-
A Narcissist who can't exercise self-restraints when it comes to acting grandiose

Mental Abuse-
Verbal threats, Gaslighting, Isolation, Smearing, Withholding and other tactics to control a person's way of thinking by destroying their self-esteem, lowering their confidence and undermining their reality

Mental Gymnastics-
When our thoughts spiral into destructive patterns where we may make up excuses or arguments for unjustifiable decisions, keeping us from positive and/or healthy actions

Mental Illness-
Emotional instability and disorder characterized by a significant disturbance in a person'e cognition, emotional regulation and/or behavior

Merry-Go-Round-
The continuous cycling of Abuse, where you stay in the relationship thinking it's going to get better, when it doesn't, but you continue and the pattern keeps repeating itself

Milestones Missed-
When Targeted Parents experience another holiday or birthday without their Alienated Child(ren)

Mind Control-
Abuser's use of forcible or deceptive tactics to influence their Target's autonomy and identity

Mind Games-
Series of deliberate and manipulative actions or responses planned to psychologically alter one's thinking

Mind Reader-
When the Narcissist seems to know what you are thinking because they have done a great deal of observation and research on their Target

Mindfuckery-
When the Abuser intentionally confuses his/her Target by destabilizing their reality

Mindfullness-
When you practice being present, aware and attentive to your thoughts and emotions

Mini-Me-
When the parent lives through one of their children, in an attempt to reclaim their own inadequacies and failed accomplishments. For example, a father whose son plays in the same position in the same sport with the same jersey number as the dad had in his youth or the mother whose daughter is being molded to be a professional ballerina because the mother studied ballet

Minion-
Someone who follows directions, cooperates with the Narcissist, provides services or intel and is agreeable to the orders given to them

Mirroring-
Abuser copies their Target's likes and dislikes and reflects the Target's personality, style and values

Misandry-
The hatred, contempt or ingrained prejudice against men

Misogyny-
The hatred, contempt or ingrained prejudice against women

Mockery-
When the Narcissist uses sarcasm or jokes that put their Target down

Model Parent-
A parent who is a positive, authentic, influencing role model for his/ her children. Alienators pretend and go to great lengths to create a False perspective that they are a Model Parent

Modified No Contact-
When you only communicate when necessary and related to urgent or serious matters

Moments of Clarity-
Small periods of time when the Abuser seems to understand the negative consequences of his/ her behavior and apologizes or tries to make amends

Monitored Visitation-
When a parent has been court-ordered to be supervised when they see their child(ren)

Monkey Branching-
Secretive dating behavior where a Narcissist continues to pursue other potential partners while already in a relationship or marriage with someone else

Monogamy-
Being married to or having intimate relations with one person at a time

Mood Swings-
Experiencing a fluctuation of emotions, ups and downs, for long periods of time

Moral Compass-
A person's ability to judge the difference between good and bad, right and wrong

Mortification-
When the Narcissist experiences humiliation and shame because his/her pride or self-respect is wounded

Mother Wounds-
The long-term consequences when a mom is absentee or has been emotionally distant or abusive

Moving The Goalposts-
Unfairly altering the conditions, rules or expectations during its course. In post-divorce court litigations, Narcissistic Abusers will continually add on new conditions to further Abuse their Target and keep the litigation going on as long as they can

Mum Clause-
A judge's ruling that something cannot be discussed in public

Munchausen Syndrome by Proxy-
Child Abusing Mental Illness where parent makes up false, exaggerated symptoms to make their child look sick to gain attention. Sometimes referred to as Factitious Disorder

NPD-Narcissistic Personality Disorder-
Psychological diagnosis for a person who lacks Empathy, is grandiose and needs admiration. They are often arrogant, charming, self-centered, manipulative and demanding

Name Calling-
When the Abuser uses profane, derogatory or dehumanizing words about the Target

Narc Bait-
When the Narcissist purposely does or says something to taunt their Target into an emotional reaction or action

Narc Free-
When you no longer allow Narcissists into your life

Narc Magnet-
Attracting a Narcissist by your lack of boundaries and your loving, forgiving and empathetic qualities

Narc Proofing-
Doing the research and work to understand and identify Narcissists so you will not let them into your life

Narcissism-
Exploitative characteristic of a self-absorbed person with grandiose delusions and exaggerated entitlement who is excessively seeking admiration and attention

Narcissist-
A person who lacks Empathy and views themselves as superior, demanding attention or special treatment

Narcissistic Abuse-
The complex, emotional or psychological mistreatment from a controlling and manipulative Abuser

<u>Narcissistic Collapse-</u>
When a Narcissist experiences failure, humiliation, discard, exposure or any other blow to their secretly fragile ego

<u>Narcissistic Dance-</u>
When you go back and forth with the Narcissist because you feel attracted to them and believe they would be a great partner. Letting the Narcissist take the lead by making them feel powerful, competent and worthy

<u>Narcissistic Fleas-</u>
When a normal-range, empathetic person starts acting like a disordered, entitled Narcissist after spending time with them

<u>Narcissistic Injury-</u>
When the Abuser feels threatened and endures emotional pain caused by rejection or exposure

<u>Narcissistic Rage-</u>
When the Abuser defensively reacts to a bruised ego with anger and aggression

<u>Narcissistic Scar-</u>
When the shame and disgrace is so significant that the Narcissist can never truly feel good about themselves, their actions and how they have hurt so many people

<u>Narcissistic Smirk-</u>
Smug facial expression when the Narcissist feels good about the pain he/she has caused the Target, or the satisfaction of knowing that they got away with deceit

<u>Narcissistic Stare-</u>
An intense, long, blank gaze at their Target used to either draw them in or reprimand them for speaking the truth or sharing their feelings

Narcissistic Supply-
The Abuser's constant need to fulfill their self-esteem needs and emptiness within them with those that provide attention, adoration and support

Narcissistic Tantrums-
Angry outbursts that are shocking and sudden, creating an uncomfortable scene, which shows the Narcissist's short temper

Narcissistic Wound-
When the Abuser feels threatened and endures emotional pain caused by rejection or exposure, and his/her ego is traumatized which devastates their pride and self-worth

Narcissus-
A figure in Greek mythology who believed himself to be so handsome, that he fell in love with his own refection. Even the nymph Echo could not temp him away from his self-absorption

Narcopath-
Shortened version of Narcissistic Sociopath, in which the Abuser reflects sadistic, evil and manipulative tendencies

Need For Closure-
The Target's motivation to achieve finality to a situation. Narcissists do not have this same need, they don't communicate the reasons their feelings have changed and they prefer ambiguity as they continue to Abuse their Targets long after the end of a relationship

Negative Self-Talk-
Target's internal dialogue reinforcing negative beliefs and fears

Negging-
Manipulation technique of Abuser's deliberate backhanded flirtatious compliments to undermine the Target's confidence, causing them to seek approval

Neglect-
Failure of caregiver to meet a person's basic needs of food, shelter and love

Neglected Child-
An Abuser's or Alienator's denial of attention, care or affections essential for a child's physical, emotional and intellectual development

Nesting-
When a parent, often the mother, focuses on creating a home in anticipation of the arrival of children; just like birds do before they lay eggs

Neurolinguistic Therapy-
Programming to change someone's thoughts and behaviors to stop ruminating on the negatives and Abuse from the Narcissist

Neurosis-
Being obsessively Anxious, moody and/or depressed

Neurotypical-
Comparing a healthy, balanced person's behavior with someone who has mental, behavioral or Narcissistic qualities

New Recruit-
The latest supply drafted into the Harem, who will align with and provide attention to the Narcissist

Nice and Nasty Cycle-
Abuser's strategy to win over the affection of their Target before they reveal their negative qualities

No Closure-
No final agreement to or communication about the ending of a relationship

No Contact-
Stopping all forms of communication and cutting ties between the Abuser and the Target

No-Win Scenario-
When the Target is forced into choosing between two negative options

Non-Custodial Parent-
A parent who does not have primary physical custody of their child(ren) due to a court order

Normal Range Parent-
A parent who loves their child and is able to instill positive values and impose reasonable, natural consequences while teaching them right from wrong

Normalizing-
Manipulation tactic Abusers use to desensitize their Target to Abusive, coercive or cruel behavior to get them to agree or accept immoral and/or harmful treatment

Not-My-Fault Syndrome-
Avoiding personal responsibility for your words and behavior, while blaming another

Numbing-
Masking our emotions to avoid the reality of the situation

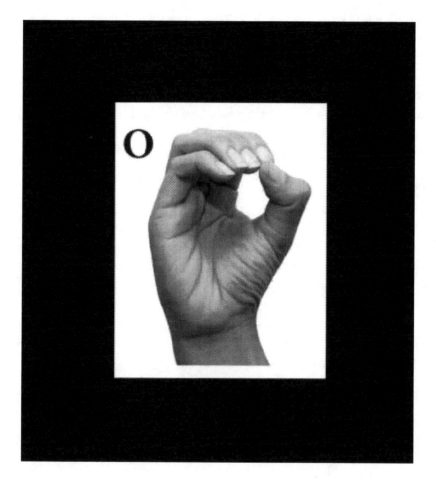

OCD-Obsessive Compulsive Disorder-
Chronic challenge where someone has uncontrollable, reoccurring thoughts or behaviors that he/ she feels the urge to repeat over and over

Object Constancy-
Abuser's inability to comprehend that a person can have both positive and negative qualities at the same time

Obsession-
Persistent, excessive thoughts or anxious impulses that take priority. Abusers often obsess over the destruction of their Targets after they have left or escaped the relationship, and continue taking them to court, filing False Accusations, Stalking and Harassment

Obsessive Compulsive-
Person who can't control their persistent thoughts and acts on them

Obsessive Love Disorder-
Psychological condition where a person has an overwhelming, repeated desire to love, protect and possess another person

One Night Stand-
Sexual encounter that happens once with someone you don't know well or don't want to continue a relationship with

One-Sided Relationship-
A connection between two people that lacks balance and equitable reciprocity, where one person is the giver and the other is the taker

Open Wound-
Emotional pain that doesn't or hasn't been healed

Oppositional Defiant Disorder-ODD-
Person who is uncooperative, defiant and hostile towards others, especially authority figures

Optics-
The facade created by the Narcissist to portray a certain False Image

Order of Protection-
Legal document where a judge orders one person to stay away from another. This can be needed to protect Targets from Abusers, however these orders can be falsely placed on innocent people by malevolent Abusers who lie and are just getting back at their ex

Ostracism-
Excluding or banishing someone from interacting with others

Othello Syndrome-
Delusional jealousy or unsubstantiated belief that your spouse is cheating

Outside Influences-
People or media that influence your perceptions

Outsmart the Narcissist-
Statements or actions that put the Narcissist in his/her place as unimportant. It's critical to understand the personality type and tactics of the Narcissist, stay one step ahead anticipating their actions, then make sure you put up Healthy Boundaries or go No Contact

Overgiver-
Either the empathetic, generous, people-pleasing Target whose gifts are over-the-top or the Narcissist could be the extreme gift giver during the Love Bombing phase

Overinflated Ego-
The Narcissist's belief that they have no flaws and are superior to others

Overstep Boundaries-
To not respect another's limits or requests, or to go beyond what is they express as comfortable

Overt Narcissist-
Self-absorbed person who very loudly displays grandiosity, entitlement and superiority

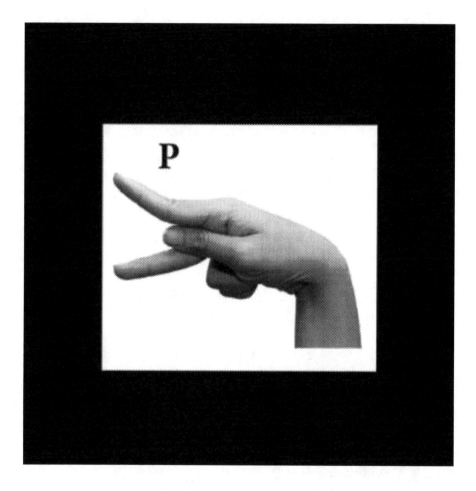

Pandora's Box-
Some situation that creates a great number of problems that you didn't expect

Panic Attack-
Sudden onset of intense anxiety and fearfulness, coupled with physical symptoms, when there is no actual danger

Parallel Parenting-
When separated or divorced parents can't work with one another and each has their own approach to parenting when the children are with them

Paranoia-
Persecutory, grandiose or anxious delusions not based in reality, but very common for Targets to experience as they have been Gaslit

Parasitic Narcissist-
An covert Abuser who deliberately manipulates and exploits good, honest people emotionally and financially, leeching onto them while making their Targets dependent

Parasympathetic Nervous System-
Our body's system that controls rest, repair, enjoyment, eating, sleeping, sexual activity and social dominance. Understanding this system helps Targets take care of themselves and heal after Abuse

Parent Access-
A parent legally having the right to spend time with their child(ren)

Parent-Child Bond-
The intense attachment, love and protective instincts between a parent and their child

Parent-Child Estrangement-
The physical and emotional separation chosen by one party between a parent and their child(ren) usually as a result of past trauma or unacceptable or Abusive behavior. Unlike Alienation, which uses the child as a weapon and is instigated by an Abusing Parent to punish the other parent

Parental Alienation-
When the Abusing parent manipulates, brainwashes and turns the children against the loving Targeted parent with outright lies, believable half-truths, indoctrination and manipulation to erase the normal-range, Loving Parent from the child's life and ensure the child aligns with them

Parental Favoritism-
When one or both parents display consistent positive attention toward one child over another

Parental Rejection-
When an Abusing Parent or caregiver denies attention, care or affection considered essential for a child's wellbeing

Parentification-
When a child takes on the reverse-role responsibility to care for their parent

Parenting App-
Technological program, sometimes court ordered, used to schedule and communicate with a volatile ex about the children

Parenting Plan-
A written outline of how, when and where the child(ren) will spend time with each parent

Parenting Style-
A parent's unique approach, attitudes, behaviors and actions towards their child(ren). Parenting styles may include: authoritarian, authoritative, permissive and uninvolved

Parenting Time-
The time a divorced parent physically spends with the child(ren)

Passive Aggressive Behavior-
Abusers pretending that they are neutral, when in fact their motives are aggressively calculated

Pathogenic Parent-
An Abusive Parent whose negative and harmful behaviors cause discord with the child(ren)

Pathological Envy/Jealousy-
Abuser's false belief that their spouse is cheating on them, when they are not

Pathological Love Relationship-
When a Target experiences inevitable harm from their Abuser

Pathological Lying-
Compulsive habit of not telling the truth

Patriarchy-
Social system where men hold the primary power and privilege within families

Patronizing-
Passive-aggressive, condescending behavior Abusers use to belittle and put down a Target while pretending to be friendly or reasonable

Patterns of Abuse-
A person's behavior, attitudes and actions used to gain and maintain power and control over another. Abuse can be physical, emotional, verbal, sexual, financial, psychological or cultural

Pawn-
The Abused, powerless child who is used as a weapon against the Targeted parent

Peace Keeper-
Someone who helps prevent or stops the fighting between others

People Pleaser-
An empath who is overly helpful and kind

Perfect Child-
Child who tries very hard to do the right things just to keep the parents happy

Perfect Family-
There is no such thing, however, Narcissists project a False Image that their family has no flaws

Perfect Parent-
There is no such thing, however, an Alienator will try to portray that their parenting is far superior than the other parent's

Perfectionist-
When Abusers demand high and excessive levels of performance from their Targets

Perjury-
Willfully lying in court after taking an oath or signing that they are telling the truth. Narcissists regularly commit perjury and are often never held accountable for their intentional deceit

Permissiveness-
Where one parent allows the child(ren) to disregard the other parent's general rules or behavioral expectations

Perpetrator-
An Abuser who engages in harmful, illegal or immoral acts

Persona-
The image that a person presents about their own character and values

Personality Disorder-
Mental Illness with patterns of abnormal thoughts or behavior

Perverse Triangle-
Where two people are against a third person. One parent could have a covert alliance with their child(ren), who band together to undermine the other parent's authority

Peter Pan Syndrome-
People who have difficulty growing up and being responsible, including maintaining healthy adult relationships

Petulant Borderline Personality Disorder-BPD-
Diagnosis for a person who exhibits dramatic mood swings, passive-aggressive behavior, irritability, low self-esteem and defiance

Physical Abuse-
Unwanted or unwarranted physical contact by an Abuser causing physical or emotional injury

Ping-Ponged-
The going back and forth or transferring from one place to another. How children feel when having to go from one divorced parent's house to the other's

Pink Cloud-
The honeymoon phase in a relationship where you feel exhilaration or euphoria

Pity-Ploy-
When someone is self-degrading and fishes for compliments, affection or for others to disregard their negative actions

Planting Seeds of Doubt-
When the Abuser drops negative and untrue hints about the Targeted person

Plausible Deniability-
When a person denies knowledge of or responsibility for the actions of others

Playbook-
The common behaviors, tactics and strategies used by Abusing Narcissists in their relationships

Player-
A Narcissist who participates in numerous relationships at the same time

Playing The Field-
A Narcissist who gets involved with numerous people at the same time

Please and Appease Response-
When you Fawn over and serve others, at your own expense, to avoid conflict and disapproval

Poisoned Children-
Children who have been Alienated by an Abuser to believe a False Narrative about their other parent

Polygamy-
Marriage to more than one spouse at the same time

Pornography-
Writings or image with exploitative sexual content; Narcissists are often obsessed with and addicted to pornography

Possessiveness-
Abuser's claim that they own the Target and the Target is their possession belonging to them

Post Traumatic Stress Disorder-PTSD-
Condition where someone has difficulty controlling their emotions after experiencing severe adversity and/or a traumatic event

Posturing-
The belief, actions and attitudes an Abuser will portray for a period of time to prove a point or align others with them

Power-
The Narcissist's dispositional need to seek to control others by any means

Power and Control Wheel-
A circle chart for advocates and victims to identify patterns of Abusive behaviors

Powerlessness-
When you feel you have no control over an outcome

Predator-
An Abuser who seeks out to exploit or cause harm to another

Predominant Aggressor-
The Abuser who poses the most serious, ongoing threat to the Target or Victim

Preferred Parent-
The Alienating, favored dad or mom, with whom the child(ren) aligns with

Premeditation-
The Abuser's planning and plotting for the Target's demise

Prey-
The Targeted Victim who is being stalked, harassed or Abused

Primary Supply-
The Narcissist's main grade A relationship

Pro-Se Litigant-
When a person represents themselves in court without a lawyer

Projection-
Abuser's defense in accusing you for what they are doing to avoid accountability

Projective Identification-
A communication strategy where the Narcissist accuses the Target of their own negative, personality Splitting

Promiscuity-
Casual sexual relations with a variety of partners. Narcissists often engage in multiple relationships

Prostitute-
A person who engages in sexual activity for payment or a Flying Monkey that does the bidding for the Narcissistic Abuser

Protection From Abuse Order-PFA-
Legal document where a judge orders a person to stay away from another. This can be needed to protect Targets from Abusers, however these orders can be falsely placed on innocent people by malevolent Abusers who lie and are just getting back at their ex

Provocativeness-
Sexual behavior intended to provoke, excite or stimulate another person

Pseudo Empathy-
Abusers pretending to care about their Targets

Pseudo Intimate-
When the Narcissist pretends to feel close and connected, but there is a lack of emotional empathy

Pseudomutuality-
Facade of happiness and perfect harmony in your relationship, which is projected to others to keep the Abuse private. The relationship appears to benefit both, but really, one is using the other for their own gain

Psychiatrist-
A medical doctor who specializes in mental health issues and is authorized to prescribe medications to treat patients with Mental Illness

Psycho-
An Abuser who violates other's rights, including breaking the law, exploitation, deceitfulness, impulsivity, aggression and irresponsibility with a lack of guilt, remorse or empathy

Psychodynamic Therapy-
Counseling focused on people's reaction to motives to help understand the unconscious mind

Psychological Abuse-
Abuser's acts of verbal, non-physical hostility against the Target

Psychological Trauma-
Damage or injury to a person's psyche after living through fear or psychological distress, including Domestic Violence, Narcissistic Abuse, Parental Alienation and/or Intergenerational Family Trauma

Psychologist-
Professional who analyzes and counsels on mental health and understanding the mind and human behavior

Psychopath-
An Abuser who violates other's rights, including breaking the law, exploitation, deceitfulness, impulsivity, aggression and irresponsibility with a lack of guilt, remorse or empathy

Psychopathy-
Impulsive disregard of social norms, while being callous to other's suffering

Psychotherapist-
A professional who uses forms of communication and interaction to assess, diagnose and treat dysfunctional reactions and behavioral patterns

Psychotic Episode-
When a person has temporary complicated and blatant behavioral symptoms such as hallucinations, delusions or disorganized speech

Public Image or Persona-

The opinion that others have about someone, related to their values and actions. Narcissists create a False Public Image or Persona and are said to wear a mask to conceal their true negative character

Punishment-

Physical or emotional consequence imposed by someone to reprimand perceived negative behavior. Abuser's will attempt to keep a False Narrative alive by punishing their ex-spouses who know the truth, escaped and may expose the Narcissist

Push-Pull-

Chronic pattern Abusers use of sabotaging and then reestablishing relationships

QDRO-Qualified Domestic Relations Order-
Court order that determines the "alternate payee's" right to receive a portion of retirement benefits payable to their ex spouse

Qualified Expert-
A person who will testify in court as someone who has knowledge, education and experience on a certain topic

Quality Supply-
A favored relationship who gives attention and admiration to the Narcissist

Quicksand-
Just when you think you can be free of the Abusing Narcissist, you are sucked back into their control, often by frivolous court petitions and legal harassment

Quid Pro Quo-
A favor or advantage granted or expected in return for something

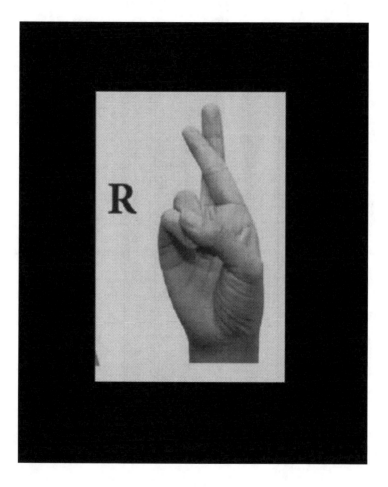

Rabbit Hole-
Metaphor for falling into a never-ending mess of issues

Radical Acceptance-
Positively acknowledging the reality of your situation and choosing to move forward by letting go of the need to change or control the outcome

Rage-
Intense, uncontrollable and/or aggressive anger

Ranked Supply-
The Narcissist's list of back up relationships, placed in an order of preference

Rape-
Non-consensual sexual penetration using force or threats

Ratio-
The initial numbers in divorce discovery that divides the assets and debts between the parties; Narcissistic or malevolent spouses will create professional-looking spreadsheets with inaccurate numbers to take financial advantage of their partners

Reactive Abuse-
The Abuser turns the tables and convinces the shamed Victim that their reaction to the Abuse is their fault and that they are the actual Abuser, causing the Victim to feel shame and guilt as they dependently rely on the Abuser's interpretation of the situation and react, as opposed to responding to reality

Reactive Attachment Disorder-
Diagnosed disorder that happens to children whose developmental and social patterns and interactions were disrupted

Rebound-
When a person jumps into another relationship right after the ending of a relationship. Targets often fall for Narcissists a second or third time

Recovered Children-
When Alienated Children are reunited with their Targeted Parent

Recovered Memories-
When you recall a previously repressed prior traumatic event, such as sexual, physical or emotional Abuse

Recruiting New Supply-
The Narcissist's efforts to connect with others he/she can have a relationship with in the future

Recycled Relationships-
Narcissists returning to their former partners for attention, control and Triangulation

Red Flags-
Signs, often missed or ignored, that someone is Abusing you

Refueling Supply-
When the Narcissist gives indications or False Hope to those he/she would like to continue a relationship with, to keep them hooked and waiting on the sidelines

Regeneration-
Becoming renewed and restored after experiencing Domestic Violence, Narcissistic Abuse, Parental Alienation and/or Intergenerational Family Trauma

Regime-
People who believe and align with your Abuser and do the dirty work bidding and gathering of information for them

Regret-
Emotional response to remembering a past experience, wishing the outcome would have been different

Rejected Child-
When a parent stops positive interactions with their own child

Rejected Family-
When an Alienated Child(ren) turns away from the Targeted Parent's side of the family

Rejected Parent-
The Loving Parent whose relationship with their child(ren) has been interfered with by the other Alienating Parent. The parent is undermined and their previously positive relationship with their child(ren) is damaged or disrupted without a valid reason or justification, usually as punishment for leaving the Abuser

Rejection-
Denial of love, attention, interest and/or approval

Relational Trauma-
Reaction involving relationships, resulting from abandonment, Abuse, bullying and/or humiliation

Relationship Dynamics-
Relationships can be healthy or unhealthy. Relationship Dynamics can also include Abusive patterns of behavior between two people that impact how they interact, communicate or relate

Relative Deprivation-
When the Alienating Parent does not allow or interferes with the child(ren) seeing to communicating with the other parent's side of the family

Remarriage-
Getting married again after divorce

Remediation-
Fixing, reversing or stopping a damaging situation

Remedy-
The court's granting of "relief" to a Victim who has been harmed by their Abuser

Remorse-
Strong sense of guilt and regret for a past action

Rendezvous-
The meeting up with an affair partner when cheating

Reparenting-
When a professional models and teaches appropriate parenting behavior

Repercussions-
The results of your decisions and actions

Repetition Compulsion-
After the Narcissist is discarded by the Target, he/she stays in the Idealization Phase, so jumping to a new supply is easy and effortless. The ex is an interchangeable external object. In the relationship, the internal objectification is what matters

Replacement Family-
When one of the parents remarry or when a child(ren) chooses to connect with someone else's family and not their own

Repressed Emotions-
The holding in and burying of your thoughts

Repressed Memories-
Unconsciously not remembering prior events

Repression-
When you hold in and don't express your thoughts and impulses

Reprogramming-
Using therapy to rewire someone's thought patterns

Research-
The study on a particular topic

Resentment-
Feelings of anger and jealously towards another person

Resilience-
The ability to bounce back after experiencing Adversity

Resources-
The number of supports available to help work through issues

Respect-
Feeling of deep admiration for someone because of their values, integrity, abilities, experience, qualities, actions or achievements

Respond, Don't React-
Thinking through your next move, as opposed to your knee-jerk actions

Restraining Order-
A court order that prohibits contact with a protected person for a period of time. Legal document where a judge orders a person to stay away from another. This can be needed to protect Targets from Abusers, however these orders can be falsely placed on innocent people by malevolent Abusers who lie and are just getting back at their ex

Retaliation-
Abuser's actions to get back at their Targets

Retraumatized-
Being traumatized all over again, by someone or something

Retribution-
Punishment inflicted on someone as vengeance for their illegal or immoral behavior

Reunification-
The restoration of the parent-child relationship after Parental Alienation

Reunification Therapy-
Psychotherapy focused on hopes of reuniting and repairing the relationship of the Targeted Parent with the Alienated Child(ren) damaged by Parental Alienation

Reunite-
Coming back together again after a period of separation

Revenge-
Inflicting harm on someone who caused you harm

Revenge Porn-
Revealing sexually explicit images or videos of someone without their permission to cause them embarrassment or distress

Revolving Door-
A situation where the same problems reoccur over and over or to indicate that a person has many partners coming in and out

Reward-Punishment-
The response to certain behaviors with positive and negative consequences

Risk Indicator Checklist-RIC-
Form used to assess Victims of Domestic Abuse

Role Modeling-
When a positive and worthy person provides inspiration and an example to another through their actions

Roller Coaster Ride-
Where things are up and then they're down, they are good and then they are bad. A Whirlwind of emotions that can leave a person feeling confused and exhausted

Rubberband-
In a relationship where a person vacillates between being close to a partner and then pulling away

Rumination-

Repeatedly thinking negative thoughts

Rumor Mill-

Negative, often false comments made about a Targeted person who is a Victim of an Abuser's Smear Campaign

Sabotage-
When the Abuser deliberately destroys, damages or obstructs for their own advantage

Sadistic Narcissist-
A person who derives pleasure from causing physical or psychological pain and suffering to others

Safe House-
Emergency, transitional or permanent confidential shelter for Targets of Abuse

Safe Parent-
The Targeted Parent who unconditionally loves their Alienated Child(ren) and would never, ever harm them

Sandbagging-
Manipulative, Abusive behavior that dupes the Target into lowering resistance or expectations, which then sets the Target up for being exploited

Sarcasm-
When the Narcissist uses mockery or jokes that put their Target down

Scammer-
A psychological Abuser who proclaims to be honest and in high moral standing, yet dupes their Targets falsely

Scapegoat Child-
The child that gets blamed for the family's dysfunction

Scarlett Letter-
When a cheater gives clues or it is evident that they have committed adultery. Previously a letter A was worn in shame for committing this immoral act

Schizoid-
A person who withdraws from social interactions and prefers to be alone

Script-
The Narcissist's very detailed fantasy and playbook

Scrolling-
The action of going through posts to gather information

Secondary Supply-
Either the person that is next in line for the Narcissist to connect with or projecting the False Image that the Narcissist is living the good life, is upwardly mobile and successful; Mr. or Mrs. B

Secret Agent-
A person with something to hide

Secret Agent Man-
Most likely your Abusing, Narcissistic husband

Secret Agent Woman-
Most likely your Abusing, Narcissistic wife

Secret Codes-
Narcissist's hidden language or efforts to hide secret information within other information so it is not readily revealed

Secret Family-
When your spouse actually has another family he/she hides while you are married

Secret Passwords-
Passwords that have codes embedded in them, such as initials, birthdays or addresses of people they've had affairs with or want to cheat with in the future

Secrets-
Information Narcissists or Abusers hide from others

Seduction Phase-
When the Narcissist is trying to win over a Target with Idealization and showering of attention, including sexual attention

Selective Amnesia-
When a person loses or chooses to lose only certain parts of their memory

Selective Memory-
The purposeful forgetting of memories for an Abuser to create a False Narrative

Self Absorbed-
The preoccupation about one's own being, often a characteristic of Narcissists

Self Actualization-
Realization that you are able, capable and worthy of living a beautiful life

Self-Aggrandizement-
The Narcissist's display and appearance of superiority through pompous behavior, boasting or bragging

Self Aware-
Attention or knowledge of themselves

Self Aware Narcissist-
A Narcissist who knows he/she has Narcissistic Personality traits

Self Blame-
Taking responsibility for an outcome, even if you are not responsible for it

Self-Care-
Activities you do to promote your well-being, especially needed after experiencing or surviving Abuse or Alienation

Self Deprecation-
Reprimanding yourself by belittling, undervaluing or disparaging yourself

Self-Destruction-
Actions that focus on the negative and prevent you from moving forward

Self-Determination-
A person's ability to choose a positive path to their life as they grow, learn and move forward

Self-Esteem-
How you feel about yourself

Self-Harm-
Pain a Target inflicts on themselves on purpose

Self Image-
One's view of themselves

Self Isolation-
Choosing to or being Gaslit to separate yourself from others or your support system

Self-Loathing-
The Narcissist's extreme hatred of who they really are

Self Love-
High regard for your own well-being and contentment

Self Sabotage-
Choosing to interfere with your own positive outcome

Self Soothing-
Actions to provide temporary relief from emotional distress

Separation-
Taking a break from a relationship, often prior to a divorce

Serial Cheater-
When your partner has multiple extramarital affairs

Settlement-
Final outcome of a divorce, however Abusers will often continue to challenge settlements in numerous post-divorce petitions as a means to continue to inflict harm on their exes

Sexism-
Beliefs based on the ideology that one gender is superior over another

Sexual Abuse-
Unwanted and inappropriate sexual contact or exploitation by an Abuser

Sexual Coercion-
When Abusers use subtle pressure, false statements, drugs or alcohol to force sexual contact with a Target against their will

Sexual Infidelity-
When a spouse or intimate partner cheats, becoming sexually involved with another person

Sexual Objectification-
The Narcissist viewing the Target as sexually useful or attractive, rather than engaging in a meaningful relationship or expression of love

Shadow Work-
Looking within to understand your role in relationship dynamics. Embracing the dark and moving towards and recognizing the light with our own growth and healing

Shame-
When you feel that your are not good enough

Shame Shifting-
Tactic used to shift the shame away from the perpetrator of Abuse and place it on the Victim

Shanda-
Yiddish term for something shameful or scandalous

Shape Shifter-
Description of how a Covert Narcissist can change his/her personality and actions to fit a different narrative or relationship

Shared Fantasies-
The Narcissist convinces or coerces their partner into believing the distorted reality of the Narcissist's grandiosity and idealized self-image

Shared Parenting-
When a divorced couple work together for the betterment of the child(ren) to split responsibilities

Shattered Dreams-
The shocking reality that your life plans are based on a False Reality and are not going to materialized as you expected or hoped

Shattered Lives-
The shocking reality that there are many people who are negatively affected by the actions of the Abuser and their cohorts

Shell Shocked-
Panicked feeling of disbelief, fear and helplessness

Shelving-
The Narcissist's act of keeping his/her Back Up Supply nearby, so they can call on these past lovers or relationships when they have the opportunity to reengage

Short Leash-
When the Abuser controls their Target and only allows them small amounts of independence or freedom

Sibling Alienation-
When an Abusive Alienating Parent programs the children to reject and denigrate each other, so they do not have a relationship or can compare notes unveiling the truth

Sibling Estrangement-
When the Alienator consciously keeps the children isolated from each other so they siblings don't have a relationship and can compare notes about their childhood experiences or views of the Targeted parent, or when a brother or sister chooses not to have a relationship with their sibling(s)

Sideline-
When a married partner has another relationship in the wings

Silenced-
When you are forced not to share the truth or suffer detrimental consequences

Silent Treatment-
Abuse tactic to punish, manipulate and control Target by stopping all forms of communication for a period of time

Silver Lining-
The often unseen positive outcome resulting from a negative situation

Slander-
Crime of making a false spoken statement that damages and defames a person's reputation

Slay the Dragon-
When the Target or Victim faces the situation involving their Abuser and overcomes their fear

Sleep Deprivation-
Abuser's tactic of routinely interrupting, impeding or restricting their Target's sleep cycle

Slut-
A woman who has many casual sexual partners

Smear Campaign-
The Abuser's gossip of telling of lies and half-truths to people close to their Target to get them to avoid, fear or disassociate with the Target so the Target loses their Support System and the Abuser gains sympathy

Smear Campaign By Proxy-
When the Abuser gets other people to gossip or tell lies and half-truths to discredit the Target and get others to avoid, fear or disengage with them so they lose their Support System of friends, family, neighbors, coworkers, acquaintances and even their own children

Smooth Criminal-
An Abuser who doesn't seem like someone who would break the law or hurt others, but does

Smother Love-
When a parent is excessive in their child's life which appears genuine, but is really the parent's need to control and manipulate the child, resulting in the child being dependent on that parent

Snake Charmer-
A Covert, Malignant Narcissist who can win over people with lies and False Narratives

Social Anxiety-
When you fear or are uncomfortable in social situations

Social Worker-
Licensed Mental Health professional who connects people with resources, and helps people and families deal with emotional, economic and familial challenges

Sociopath-
An Abuser who violates other's rights, including breaking the law, exploitation, deceitfulness, impulsivity, aggression and irresponsibility with a lack of guilt, remorse or empathy

Sole Custody-
When a parent has a court order that the child(ren) are 100% within their care. Narcissistic Alienators often fight for this, even though the other parent was the primary caregiver for years and the Alienator really doesn't want to take care of the child(ren)

Somatic Narcissist-
A Narcissist who is physically driven to believe that they are superior

Soul Mate-
A loving person who you have a deep connection with. Narcissists pretend to be this

Spell-
Trance-like state that Abusers use to persuade their Targets

Spiritual Abuse-
When an Abuser uses spirituality or religion to exert power and control over a Target

Spiritual Awakening-
A turning point when you realize there are bigger, non-human forces influencing the universe

Spiritual Narcissist-
A person who uses faith, religion and/or spirituality to manipulate others and get Narcissistic Supply to boost their own ego

Splitting-
Protective defense mechanism where a person can't integrate opposing situations resulting from Abuse or Trauma. In Parental Alienation, children's personality becomes split when a child looks at one parent as all-good and the other as all-bad

Spying-
Secretly tracking another or covertly looking into something to get information

Stalking-
When the Abuser pursues, follows or harasses a Target

Status Quo-
The general state of things or situations that are unchallenged

Stealing-
Taking assets that don't belong to you

Stepfamily-
The second blended family that results when one parent remarries someone and has a family with them or who already has a family

Stigmatized-
Being unfairly and negatively regarded by others

Stockholm Syndrome-
Loyalty and psychologically aligning with and trusting your Abuser. Term taken from bank robbery in Stockholm, Sweden where the hostages developed feelings for and defended their Abusive captors

Stolen Children-
Alienated or abducted children from an Abuser. Parental Alienation involves an Alienating Abusive Parent stealing the child(ren) away from the Targeted, Loving Parent

Stolen Home-
When the Narcissist takes your family house either outright or by deceptive means, such as forging and fraudulent documents and actions

Stonewalling-
Refusal to engage in a conversation or provide information as a form of punishment

Stringing You Along-
Keeping you hooked by Future Faking promises, Intermittent Reinforcement and/or Trauma-Bonding

Stunted Emotional Growth-
The inability or reluctance to learn from your mistakes, improve your coping strategies and flourish emotionally

Submission-
Compliance with or surrender to your Abuser's requests or demands

Substance Abuse-
The misuse of drugs and alcohol

Sugar Daddy-
A wealthy man who lavishes gifts on a woman in return for her company or sexual favors

Suicidal Ideation-
Thoughts or preoccupation with killing yourself

Superiority Complex-
Narcissistic, entitled beliefs that you are better than others and deserve special treatment

Supervised Visits-
When a parent has been court-ordered to be monitored when they see their child(ren)

Supply-
The Abuser's collection of admirers who feed their ego

Support System-
The group of people who understand your situation and have your back

SurThriver-
An Abuse Victim who not only survives the Abuse, but goes on to live a better life as a result

Survivor-
A person who got through Abuse

Survivor's Guilt-
The unworthy feelings that Victims experiences after surviving Abuse or harm, where they believe that more could have been done or that they shouldn't have come through their ordeal if others don't survive

Survivor's Voice-
Being able to speak or write about your Abuse ordeal

Suspicion-
Feeling of cautious distrust that something is possible, likely, true or already happened

Swindler-
Calculating Abuser who sets out to obtain your money, investments and assets

Swinger-
Spouse who engages in swapping partners or engaging in various forms of sexual activities with others outside of the marriage

Taboo-
Religious, moral or social conventions prohibiting certain forbidden behaviors

Taking Sides-
When some outside party chooses to align with one and not the other

Taking the Bait-
Falling for the Abuser's manipulation or intentional set up

Talk Therapy-
Psychological counseling using verbal interactions and treatment

Target-
The person the Abuser or Alienator is against

Targeted Parent-
The Loving Parent whose relationship with their child(ren) has been interfered with, undermined, damaged or disrupted without a valid reason or justification, usually as vindictive punishment for leaving the Abuser

Targeted Spouse-
The normal-range spouse who is the subject of Abuse from the Narcissistic spouse

Temporary Restraining Order-
A short-term legal PFA-Protection From Abuse Order which is used to prevent an Abuser from contacting or being near a Victim

Tertiary Supply-
A third person in line for the Narcissist to fall back on if the primary and secondary supply is not available

Testing-
When the Abuser forces their Target to repeatedly prove their loyalty

Thanatophobia-
Fear of losing your loved ones

Therapeutic-
Having a beneficial or curative effect

Thought Policing-
Any process of trying to question, control or influence a Target's ideas or feeling

Threats-
When the Abuser demonstrates intent to inflict harm to a Target

Thriver-
Targeted Abuse Victim who goes on to work through the Abuse and adversity to live a positive life

Throw Bones-
Positive actions of or gifts from a Narcissist to keep their Targeted Supply hooked through Intermittent Reinforcement

Tough Love-
A parent's strategy to stop enabling and rewarding their child's unhealthy behavior, enforcing Healthy Boundaries and encouraging them to act responsibly

Toxic Amnesia-
The Narcissist's selective memory

Toxic Ex-
A former partner or spouse whose behavior was malevolent and Abusive

Toxic Masculinity-
When the male Narcissist is overly aggressive, domineering and controlling

Toxic Romanticism-
An unhealthy relationship based on false romantic efforts

Toxic Shame-
A feeling that you are worthless because of the poor treatment from others

Toxic Stress-
Prolonged anxiety that emotionally, physically and cognitively disrupts brain development

Toxicity-
Behavior of an Abuser that has a negative or harmful effect on a Victim

Track and Troll-
When the Abuser or Alienator follows your every move and regularly looks you up on public sites and platforms. Alienators keep tabs on their children with spyware, air tags or controlling/paying for their electronics, phone bills, Location Services and subscriptions

Trafficking-
Illegal transportation and trade in people or commodities

Transference-
The redirection of emotions and thoughts from one person towards another person

Transgenerational-
Across many family generations

Transient Narcissism-
A self-absorbed person's displaying of Narcissistic Traits to a wide variety of people and places

Trapped-
Being stuck or forced to stay in an Abusive situation

Trauma-
Experiencing an event that causes emotional stress or physical injury

Trauma Bond-
An emotional connection between yourself and your Abuser which allows the unhealthy dynamic to continue

Traumatic Grief-
Ruminating response to loss, often happens to Targeted Parents who grieve the death of their living child(ren) as a result of Parental Alienation

Triangulation-
The Abuser creating competition by adding a third party into the relationship dynamic to make the Narcissist appear in high demand, causing jealousy as the Target is Gaslit

Tribalism-
When a group of people band together to exaggerate and support the False Public Image of the Narcissist or Abuser

Trickle Truths-
The Abuser slowly giving selective information, but still withholding facts so the Target is confused

Triggers-
Anything that brings up painful feelings or memories

Trophy Child-
The Narcissist's offspring who is not encouraged to follow their own independent interests, and used for show as a way of fulfilling the Abusing Parent's desires or unaccomplished past goals

Trophy Spouse-
A married partner who is regarded as "arm candy" for their status, looks and perceived success

True Colors-
The revealing of a person's real disreputable character and dishonorable motivations

Trust Issues-
Difficulty relying on the confidence and dependability of someone or something

Truth Teller-
Someone who does not lie and speaks honestly

Tunnel Vision-
Only focusing on one priority, while ignoring everything else

Twin Flame-
The belief that another person has an intense soul connection with you

Twisted Truth-
Something told that is believable but is not 100% correct, as important facts are omitted and the statements often includes half-lies

Tyrannical Sadism-
An Abuser who relishes menacing and brutalizing their Targets, forcing them to submit to their wishes and accept their intentionally destructive, inhumane and accusatory actions

Ultimatum-
A strong, final and threatening demand

Unconditional Love-
Feelings of deep affection with no expectations or strings attached

Uncover The Truth-
Finding out about your ex's or other's False Narrative or lies

Undermined-
The Narcissist's subtle putting down of another person to boost their sense of self

Undervalued-
Not believed worthy by another

Undue Hardship-
When your ex continually uses the court system to force you into financial loss as a result of fighting for justice

Undue Influence-
A form of mind control with deceptive tactics to convince a Target to put themselves in a vulnerable position to be exploited and manipulated

Unequal Justice-
Unfair legal results not based on facts, fairness or an equitable resolution

Unfaithful-
When someone cheats on their spouse or partner

Unfriending-
When someone blocks another on social media

Unfulfilled Promises-
Future Faking commitments that are not followed through with

Unilateral Divorce-
When only one spouse files for divorce without the consent of the other spouse

Unilateral Parenting-
When only one parent makes decisions without the other parent's input

Uninvolved Parent-
A parent who does not care or participate in their child's development or activities

Unmask-
Exposing the Narcissist for the malevolent, misleading person they are. In time, Narcissists often expose themselves by slipping up and unintentionally confessing to a wrongdoing

Unsupervised Visits-
Child custody times when a parent doesn't have to be monitored by someone else

Upgrade Supply-
When the Narcissist believes he/she can do better than the person they are currently in a relationship with

Upstander-
Someone who speaks out against wrongdoing, as opposed to ignoring it or choosing to stand by without speaking up or acting on the injustice

Upstanding Public Image-
Narcissist's False Persona displayed to those around him/her to make them look better and more moral than they actually are

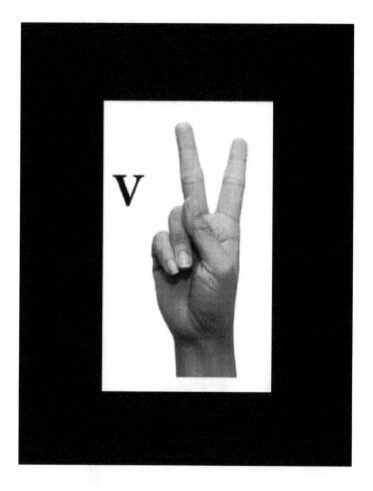

Vacant Stare-
The look an Abuser with a lack of Empathy has, like there is no deep thought or intention

Validation-
Process of establishing the truth, confirming the facts or logical agency of something

Vampire-
An Abuser who sucks the life out of their Target

Vengeful-
Seeking to harm another person in return for a perceived injury

Verbal Abuse-
When an Abuser uses words, name calling, putdowns and/or humiliation to maintain power and control to harm or weaken the Target

Verbal Threats-
When the Abuser eludes with words that they will cause you harm

Vicarious Trauma-
The impact of exposure to extreme events resulting in a person feeling Triggered or stressed about their own experiences

Victim-
The Targeted person who is Abused, harmed or killed by an Abuser

Victim Blaming-
Placing fault on the person who has been Abused

Victim Card-
Abuser's tactic to gain sympathy from others with the ulterior motive of excusing their behavior

Victim Complex-
The belief that you are always the victim and have no control over your responses. Personality trait that leads others to believe that someone is being perpetually and wrongly victimized by the harmful actions of others

Victim Shaming-
Abuser making the Victim or Target feel bad for what the Abuser has done

Victimhood-
The act or process of targeting a person for cruel or unfair treatment as a result of physical or emotional Abuse

Vigilance-
When the Victim or Target must be on the lookout for possible harm from the Abuser

Villain-
An Abuser or negative person whose evil actions or motives are the driving force for their criminal or immoral behavior

Vindictive-
Actions or thoughts of harming another due to a strong desire for revenge

Vindictive Narcissist-
A Narcissist who holds grudges, resentments and anger towards a Target and seeks revenge

Violate Custody-
When a parent does not follow the court order regarding the living arrangements for the child(ren)

Violate Orders-
When one person does not follow the legal resolution

Virtue Signalling-
When the Narcissist publicly expresses his/her morals to try to portray that they are an honorable, upstanding person so they can be believed and admired

Visitation-
The time a divorced parent is physically allowed to spend with the child(ren)

Visitation Plan-
A written outline of how the child(ren) will spend time with each parent

Void of Empathy-
Someone, often a Narcissist, who is not able to feel emotions or pain of others

Vulnerable Child-
Alienated Child(ren) who are being pressured through emotional or psychological manipulation

Vulnerable Narcissist-
Inadequate Abusers who need excessive validation from others

Vultures-
People who swoop in to take advantage of you after you've experienced Domestic Violence, Narcissistic Abuse, Parental Alienation and/or Intergenerational Family Trauma

Wake Up Call-
When the Target finally pays attention to the Red Flags of Abuse

Walking on Eggshells-
Metaphor for the emotional anxiety Targets anticipate from their Abuser

Warning Signs-
Red Flags to indicate that you are in an unhealthy relationship or situation

Wash, Rinse, Repeat Cycle-
Idiom for the cycle of repeated behaviors displayed by Abusing Narcissists

Weak Boundaries-
The inability to stand up for yourself, say "no" and demand respect from others

Weaponizing the Children-
Parental Alienation strategy when the Abusing Parent uses the child(ren) to fight and destroy the other parent

Web of Lies-
Dishonest statements that overlap and are connected with even more dishonest statements

Welfare of the Children-
What is best for the kids of divorce or separation; Unfortunately, the courts don't always get this right and award custody to the Abusing, Alienating Parent

White Knight-
When you get swept off your feet and believe someone to be your perfect soul mate. Who the Narcissist acts like during the Idealization or Love Bombing Phase early in the relationship

Whore-
A person who engages in sexual activity for payment or a Flying Monkey that does the bidding for the Narcissistic Abuser

Wishful Thinking-
The continual hoping that things will get better

Withhold Affection-
Strategy of deliberately not providing intimacy or expressing love and affection used by Narcissists to create a longing in you for them and to punish and control you

Withholding-
Keeping something or someone from another

Witness Protection Program-
Court appointed security provided to a threatened and/or Abused Victim

Wolf in Sheep's Clothing-
An Abuser who appears friendly and harmless, but is really malevolent and hostile

Womanizer-
A man who engages in numerous casual sexual affairs with women

Word Salad-
The Abuser's use of circular language and excessive terminology meant to confuse their Target

Wounded-
Injured by Abuse

Wounded Healer-
A person who helps others or is an advocate bringing awareness to Abuse because they have experienced or are currently experiencing Abuse

Wounded Self-
The false belief that we have about ourselves due to experiencing Abuse

X Your Ex-
When a Victim of Abuse decides to permanently separate from their spouse or partner

Xenophobia-
A strong and irrational fear of strangers or hostile/aggressive behavior towards others who are unlike them

Xenophobic-
A person who is pathologically afraid of strangers, often seen with children who are regulars in the foster care system

Yellow Rock-

Similar to Grey Rock where your response is boring and with no emotion, but this communication method involves being nice, friendlier and warmer to your Abuser to keep the peace

Yo-Yo Effect-

A relationship cycle where couples split up and separate, just to get back together again

Zero Contact-
Stopping all forms of communication and cutting ties between the Abuser and the Target

Zombie-
Person who is in a trance-like state who is numb to events or unreactive to treatments of them

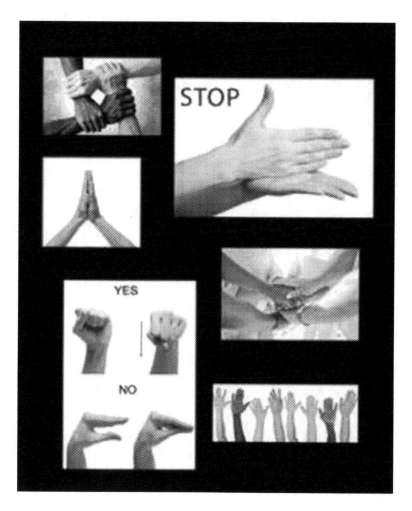

"Words are singularly the most powerful force available to humanity. We can choose to use this force constructively with words of encouragement, or destructively using words of despair. Words have energy and power with the ability to help, to heal, to hinder, to hurt, to harm, to humiliate and to humble."
~ Yehuda Berg

Check out the other books in the
TRUE DECEIT FALSE LOVE
series!